# vladislav khodasevich

*selected poems*

# vladislav khodasevich

## selected poems

translated by PETER DANIELS

introduction by MICHAEL WACHTEL

*bilingual edition*

THE OVERLOOK PRESS / ARDIS
NEW YORK, NY

This edition first published in hardcover in the United States in 2014 by
The Overlook Press / Ardis Publishers, Peter Mayer Publishers, Inc.

141 Wooster Street
New York, NY 10012
www.overlookpress.com

For bulk and special sales, please contact sales@overlookny.com,
or write us at the address above.

Library of Congress Cataloging-in-Publication Data
Khodasevich, V. F. (Vladislav Felitsianovich), 1886-1939, author.
[Poems. Selections. English. 2014]
Selected poems / Vladislav Khodasevich ; translated by Peter Daniels ; introduction by
Michael Wachtel. -- Bilingual edition.
pages ; cm
Includes bibliographical references and index.
ISBN 978-1-4683-0810-5
I. Daniels, Peter, 1954- translator. II. Wachtel, Michael, writer of added commentary.
III. Khodasevich, V. F. (Vladislav Felitsianovich), 1886-1939. Poems. Selections. 2014.
IV. Title.
PG3476.K488A2 2014
891.71'3--dc23
2013039649

Book design and type formatting by Ray Perry, Morley St Botolph, Norfolk

Manufactured in the United States of America

ISBN: 978-1-4683-0810-5

First Edition

1 3 5 7 9 10 8 6 4 2

I dream above all else of seeing Petersburg again and my friends there, and in general – Russia, exhausting, murderous, disgusting, but wondrous still, as it has been at all times.

*Autobiographical fragment*
*July 1922, Berlin*


somehow I grafted the classic rose
to the Soviet briar bush.

*'Petersburg',*
*12 December 1925, Chaville*

# Содержание

## ИЗБРАННЫЕ СТИХОТВОРЕНИЯ

# Contents

## SELECTED POEMS

# Introduction

## by MICHAEL WACHTEL

'Poetry is an extremely individualistic art, it resents isms.'
JOSEPH BRODSKY

THANKS to an abundance of translations, the names of Osip Mandelshtam, Marina Tsvetayeva, Anna Akhmatova and Boris Pasternak are familiar to non-Russian readers. Their poetry has achieved international renown, giving them pride of place in the pantheon of twentieth-century Russian literature. The same cannot be said for their contemporary Vladislav Khodasevich (1886–1939). He was an outstanding poet, but his poems are known to the English-speaking world only in piecemeal translations of variable quality published in anthologies and journals over decades. The present substantial and representative volume thus does more than fill a lacuna; it rectifies a major injustice. A great pleasure awaits the Anglophone reader.

Vladimir Nabokov once said that foreigners can't hope to understand a writer whose name they can't pronounce. So: Khodasévich. *Kh* corresponds quite closely to the *ch* in German *ich*. (But the *ch* at the end of the transliterated name is pronounced like an English *ch*, i.e. as in the word 'itch.') In the Russian language, accented syllables are particularly prominent because secondary stress does not exist. No matter how long a word, there can be only one stress, and most unstressed vowels are reduced. So the first two syllables of our poet's name sound like *uh* and *ah*, leaving the single emphatic stress to fall on the third syllable: *se*, which is pronounced something like the English 'say'. In a rough approximation: *Khuh – dah –* SAY *– vitch*.

What's in a name? For a poet, quite a bit. Khodasevich's first major collection of verse is called 'The Way of the Seed', and that seed or grain of wheat refers to John 12:24: 'Verily, verily, I say unto you, Except a corn of wheat fall into the ground and die, it abideth alone: but if it die, it bringeth forth much fruit.' This passage has a special resonance in the Russian cultural tradition, because it serves as the epigraph to Dostoyevsky's monumental final novel, *The Brothers Karamazov.*

When Khodasevich takes it into his own orbit in the profound yet laconic opening poem of his collection, he builds on the principle of biblical parable, explicitly likening the seed to many other things: first his own soul, then his country and people, and finally all living things. Another biblical parable – that of the sower – is surely not too far in the background, with the poetic word serving the function of the divine logos. The date that Khodasevich placed beneath the poem (23 December 1917) introduces a political dimension, the October Revolution. Like so many intellectuals of the time, Khodasevich was shocked by the brutality of the uprising, but hoped – vainly, as would soon become clear – to see it followed by a period of spiritual renewal. However, the first two words of the Russian poem make this national, historical and mythical fate intensely personal: *Prok*ноd*it* sаy*atel'* ('the sower goes'). Those capitalized letters, marking the stressed sylla-bles, are none other than the key sounds of the poet's own surname.[1] In short, in a 'programmatic' poem that moves in a mere twelve lines from the personal to the universal, the poet subtly opens with the most powerful signifier at his disposal: his own name.

Just as Khodasevich encrypted his name in one of his most philo-sophical poems, so he did not hesitate to incorporate his biography more generally into his verse. Strictly speaking, Khodasevich was Russian neither on his maternal nor on his paternal side. His maternal grandfather was a Jewish convert to Catholicism, while his parents were Polish. This latter inheritance is the subject of one of his greatest poems, 'The Dactyls'. In the poem 'I was born in Moscow. . .', Khoda-sevich defines his relationship to Russia as that of a 'stepson' (the Russian word has distinctly negative connotations), yet his relation-ship to Poland is still more distanced.[2] It might seem ironic that such an 'outsider' saw himself as the rightful heir and standard-bearer of the Russian poetic language. But Khodasevich's claim to Russianness rests on both language and personal history. As he contends in the poem 'Not my mother. . .', he imbibed the Russian spirit in the milk of his Russian peasant wet-nurse. (The role of this wet-nurse trans-parently parallels that of the nanny who introduced Pushkin to 'true' Russian culture through songs and folk tales.)

Khodasevich was not only born in Moscow; he grew up there, and went to school and university there (not finishing the latter, which he appears never to have taken seriously). He was living in Moscow at the

---

[1] To my knowledge this extraordinary patterning was first noted by Sergey Davydov.
[2] Khodasevich spoke fluent Polish and knew Polish literature well, but he always felt his native tradition to be Russian.

time of the October Revolution and remained there for the next two years. The devastation and misery of that era is reflected in many poems, perhaps most memorably in the magnificent blank verse meditation 'The House'. Shortly thereafter, he moved to Petersburg, where, as one of the foremost poets of the day and protected by Maksim Gorky, he served in the Soviet artistic bureaucracy and received a room in the newly created House of the Arts. This was an extraordinarily fertile period in his creative life, but by 1922 he had recognized the futility of working within the Soviet system. His emigration doomed his writings to oblivion in his native land; and, like most poets, he did not fare much better abroad. After initial wanderings in Europe, with lengthy stops in Germany and Italy, and briefly Northern Ireland, he spent the last fifteen years of his life in Paris, a period of increasing gloom, with his poetic output tapering off to nothing. To some extent, we are compensated for this absence of verse by the significant number of excellent critical prose pieces and memoirs,[3] but Khodasevich clearly felt that his poetic voice had ceased to exist by the time of his death. In the words of Nina Berberova, his companion for ten years in emigration: 'He stopped writing verse because there was no one with whom and for whom he could continue.'[4]

Despite the fact that much of it had initially appeared in the early revolutionary years, Khodasevich's poetry was not reprinted or studied until the very end of the Soviet period; the first posthumous edition was published in 1989. In the West, Khodasevich has always had champions in the Russian émigré community and among Slavists, but translators have tended to bypass his work. Two American Slavists, John E. Malmstad and Robert P. Hughes, have produced an outstanding annotated edition of Khodasevich's verse, published initially in 1983 and republished in revised and expanded form in Russia in 2009 as the first of eight planned volumes of Khodasevich's work.[5] This edition, on which Peter Daniels bases his translations, has likewise informed the present essay.

---

[3] Khodasevich's essay on Gorky, which has been translated into English, gives a good sense of his gift as a memoirist. See Donald Fanger (trans. and ed.), *Gorky's Tolstoy and Other Reminiscences* (Yale University Press, 2008), pp. 223–59.
[4] Cited from Robert P. Hughes, 'Khodasevich: Irony and Dislocation: A poet in exile', in Simon Karlinsky and Alfred Appel, Jr (eds), *The Bitter Air of Exile: Russian Writers in the West 1922–1972* (University of California Press, Berkeley, 1977), p. 65.
[5] Vladislav Khodasevich, *Sobraniye sochineniy v vos'mi tomakh*, vol. 1: *Polnoye sobraniye stikhotvoreniy* (Russkiy put', Moscow, 2009), the only volume of this edition to be devoted to poetry.

The German scholar Siegfried Krakauer coined the term *Gleichzeitigkeit des Ungleichzeitigen* (roughly, 'simultaneity of the non-simultaneous') to describe a ubiquitous yet rarely appreciated cultural phenomenon. We tend to see artistic movements as a sequence, e.g. Classicism ends and Romanticism begins, Realism ends and Symbolism begins, Symbolism ends and the Avant-garde begins. Reality, as Krakauer recognized, is much messier. Classicism overlaps with Romanticism, Realism with Symbolism, and so on. In short, linear development is a retrospective construction; contemporaries tend to experience a blur – or even a battle – of competing styles and movements.

If temporal distance encourages us to oversimplify the diversity of creativity in earlier epochs, it also frees us from their polemics, giving us a broader and less biased (because less invested) perspective. In Germany of the late nineteenth century, music was perceived as moving in two fundamentally incompatible directions, embodied by the two great composers of the age, Brahms and Wagner. So strong was the tension between these opposing forces that young composers, and listeners, were expected to choose between them. One could approve of Brahms or Wagner, but not both. Today we look back on these high-pitched battles with bemusement or even amusement. Not only is it possible to enjoy both composers; in our historical memory, they both fit under the rubric of Romanticism. Still, one need not be a trained musicologist to recognize that Wagner and Brahms represented different paths of musical development. These differences remain palpable, but time has allowed us to reconcile what was initially thought to be incompatible.

In Russia, the first two decades of the twentieth century were a time of extreme artistic diversity and accomplishment. If Russian poets of the early 1890s had little to show for themselves beyond a derivative hodgepodge of French Symbolism and Decadence, by the early years of the new century the situation had changed radically. A vibrant new type of Symbolism had come into its own, distancing itself from its French 'origins' and becoming a major cultural force with distinctively Russian obsessions. These Symbolists (Andrey Bely, Aleksandr Blok, Vyacheslav Ivanov) rejected mere aestheticism, extending their purview to all spheres of intellectual activity. Symbolism became a mystical world-view, a means of cognizing and – according to its most fervent proponents – creating reality. In short, art was no longer mere decorative expression, 'simply art', it was something that guided one's very existence. The Symbolists' vision of creativity was enormously influential, extending beyond poetry to music, philosophy and religious thought. However, the movement was always beset by contradictions and internal crises. By the end of the decade, it lost its hegemony, and Russian culture splintered into a host of schools and movements, some radically avant-garde, others more traditional in their orientation. Krakauer could hardly have found a better example of his *Gleichzeitigkeit des Ungleichzeitigen*. In poetry, the remaining Symbolists vied with the Acmeists (Nikolay Gumilyov, Anna Akhmatova, Osip Mandel'shtam) and the Futurists (Vladimir Mayakovsky, Velimir Khlebnikov) to define the nature and future of verse. The differences between these schools are so vast that it is difficult to conceive that they were occurring within the same century. Yet the same statement could be made about the work of their coevals in other areas. In the visual arts, the stylized Art Nouveau of Alexandre Benois and his World of Art brethren coexisted with the powerful realism of Ilya Repin as well as with the non-objective Suprematism of Kazimir Malevich. In music, Igor Stravinsky was developing his folk-loric and neo-primitivist idiom while Alexander Skryabin composed mystically inspired synaesthetic visions and Sergey Rakhmaninov revelled in the lush tonalities of Romanticism.

This creative ferment coincided with Khodasevich's formative years. As he himself recognized, had he been born a decade earlier, he would have inevitably been a Symbolist. Andrey Bely, five years his senior and one of the foremost Symbolists, numbered among his close friends. And, indeed, many Symbolist elements can be found in Khodasevich's work, from his basic conception of poetry as an attempt to locate the transcendent within the quotidian (see his justly celebrated *Ballada* ['Ballad of the Heavy Lyre' in Peter Daniels' translation] or 'I watch the humble working men') to his fascination with the craft of verse and the technical perfectionism it entailed. Nonetheless, Khodasevich was by nature too much of a sceptic to accept fully the mystical assumptions that guided Symbolist thought. Rather than immerse himself in esoteric doctrines, he sought inspiration in the Russian language itself, more particularly in the classics of Russian poetry.

For Khodasevich, Pushkin was an unerring authority on all things Russian. His immersion in Pushkin's work started early and never ceased. Pushkin's poetic culture is reflected throughout his writings, not only in the verse but also in a number of insightful scholarly essays that focus at times on poetics, at times on biography. When Khodasevich was asked to put together an anthology of Russian lyric poetry, he chose not to be 'representative', but to select only the finest work. 'The reader should not lament the fact that in this collection there are many works that invariably find their way into all anthologies. What can be done? We did not dare to reject poems of genius simply because their brilliance is recognized by everyone. That is why, for example, we gave so much space to Pushkin, 'the sun of Russian poetry'. After all, much space is taken up by the sun in our solar system!'[6] When criticized by the Futurist Nikolay Aseyev for an unusual grammatical construction in his poetry, Khodasevich defended himself by citing the same usage in Pushkin's verse, concluding: 'I would prefer "not to know" the Russian language like Pushkin than "to know" it like Aseyev.'[7] In 'I was born in Moscow. . .', Khodasevich locates his homeland in 'eight little volumes' – the eight-volume Pushkin edition considered authoritative at the time the poem was composed.

Khodasevich was not a prolific poet. He wrote prose with apparent ease, but poetry came slowly and often only after painstaking revision. His poetic reputation rests mainly on his three final collections, all on a very high level, and all published after the Revolution: *The Way of the Seed* (1920, Moscow; second edition 1921, Prague), *The Heavy Lyre* (1922, Moscow and Prague; second edition 1923, Berlin), and *European Night* (which never appeared as a separate book, but only as a section of the poet's collected poetry published in Paris in 1927). The titles of these collections suggest difficulty, darkness and death, and as such contrast with *Youth* and *Happy Little House*, the two books of poetry that Khodasevich published in prerevolutionary Russia (in 1908 and 1914) and later dismissed as juvenilia (but in fact even the first two books are not nearly as sunshiny as the titles suggest). None of these five books is particularly long. The present volume of translations reflects Khodasevich's – and posterity's – sense of his accomplishments; the vast majority of the poems are taken from the last three collections.

Khodasevich's poetic greatness lies in his untiring and at times heroic quest to find meaning in the world, or, to borrow one of his own images, to discern poetry in the prose of life. At times this search ends in failure and is accompanied by bitter irony.[8] At other times an epiphanic moment comes as a surprise to the poet himself. Throughout, the poet is a solitary figure navigating an unsympathetic and even hostile world. In such circumstances, the difficulty of the poet's task is magnified. Though Khodasevich regarded poetry as the highest calling, he does not idealize himself in his verse; nor does he set himself apart

---

[6] This introductory essay, written in 1914, is included in Khodasevich, 2009, p. 604.

[7] *Ibid.*, p. 410.

[8] David Bethea, author of the first (and to this date only) monograph on Khodasevich, views him as the quintessential 'ironic' poet: *Khodasevich: His life and art* (Princeton University Press, 1983).

from his fellow man, in the antagonistic relationship of 'the poet and the mob' familiar from Pushkin's famous poem so titled. Much as he might like to 'live alone' (Pushkin's advice in the sonnet 'To the Poet'), Khodasevich is incapable of ignoring the world around him. This distinguishes him both from his Symbolist forebears, who concentrated on the ideal that lay beyond the 'coarse cover of materiality' (Vladimir Solovyov's influential formulation), and from his contemporaries the Acmeists, who – at least according to their programme – celebrated 'the world below'. The speaker of Khodasevich's poetry may wish to disregard the pettiness and ugliness of his surroundings in favour of the transcendent, but this is simply not possible. When the physical world makes an appearance in Symbolist poetry, it is as a rule undifferentiated and generic, akin to the role that nature plays in a Dostoyevsky novel. In contrast, Khodasevich records the mundane with painterly precision. His method is metonymic; he focuses on a single telling detail rather than sketching a scene in broad strokes. The poem 'Petersburg', which occupies a position of special prominence by virtue of its opening his final collection, was written in emigration and looks retrospectively at the postrevolutionary years spent in Russia's once splendid capital city. It is a metapoetic poem, which closes on an uncharacteristic note of pride in poetic accomplishment. However, the effect of this final stanza owes much to the previous one, where the poet describes himself carrying 'a foul-smelling cod' through the dilapidated city. It would make little sense to seek a literary or symbolic source for this image or even to treat it as a metaphor. It is surely based on genuine experience, a piece of Soviet *realia* that forced its way into the poem, just as it had forced its way into the poet's life. Yet sandwiched between two stanzas about poetic inspiration, this unappetizing fish makes all the difference. The contiguity of the sublime and the ridiculous produces a chiaroscuro effect, no less effective in Khodasevich's verse than in Rembrandt's paintings.[9]

While a host of poetic schools battled for supremacy, Khodasevich stood apart from the fray. In an age that favoured grand gestures and utopian solutions, poets tended to speak as hierophants or prophets, declaiming their verse 'in full voice' (Mayakovsky's phrase). To this sound and fury Khodasevich responded indirectly and *sotto voce*. His restrained and understated tone was frequently misunderstood. In an overview of contemporary Russian poetry written in 1923, the brilliant and erudite critic Yury Tynyanov reproached Khodasevich

---

[9] The comparison of Khodasevich and Rembrandt was made by Andrey Bely in a 1922 essay entitled 'Rembrandt's Truth in Our Time'.

for his detached stance and rejected his poetic voice as 'not genuine'. One of the leading Russian formalists, Tynyanov favoured art that broke the rules, that challenged the familiar. Himself an authority on Pushkin, he felt that a contemporary poet should be polemically responding to Pushkin. Not surprisingly, he took Khodasevich to task for his acceptance of and reliance on the poetic culture of an earlier time. Khodasevich's poetry 'does not belong to the verse culture of our era,' he complained. Tynyanov was fully cognisant of his own prejudices. 'This does not mean that Khodasevich does not have "good"and even "excellent" poems. He does, and in twenty years it is possible that a critic will say that we have undervalued Khodasevich. Such "undervaluations" by contemporaries are always a dubious point. Their "blindness" is completely conscious ... We consciously undervalue Khodasevich because we want to see *our* poetry; this is our right.'[10]

If a poet's immersion in the culture of a previous age struck the principled Tynyanov as irresponsible escapism, no less a master of Russian letters than Vladimir Nabokov would see the matter differently. For Nabokov, Khodasevich was the 'greatest Russian poet of our time'.[11] Here one sees in a nutshell the extent to which poetic evaluation reflects a broader aesthetic stance. Nabokov viewed Pushkin as Russia's greatest poet and could likewise only admire a poet who chose to build upon this legacy. He recognized Khodasevich's numerous references to Pushkin (citations, intonations, motifs, metres) as both a homage and a mark of continuity, a conversation among generations taking place in the only homeland that was still intact. Particularly in the chaos of the postrevolutionary years, this continuity was a source of pride, an assurance that the vigour of Russian intellectual life had not been entirely lost. For Nabokov, whose own translation and commentary to *Eugene Onegin* should likewise be understood as an act of homage, this ability to discern the eternal in the fleeting was the highest praise for a poet. For Tynyanov, however, who accepted and even valued the flux of the times, Pushkin's genius lay in his dynamism. His legacy was not a 'thing' (a turn of phrase, a precise image) but rather an approach to poetic composition: 'Were Pushkin and Baratynsky alive today, they would probably keep their principles of construction, but abandon their poetic formulae.'

---

[10] These quotations are all from the third section of Tynyanov's essay 'Promezhutok' ('The Interval'), cited here according to Yury Tynyanov, *Istoriya literatury. Kritika* (Azbuka-klassika, St Petersburg, 2001), pp. 404–06.

[11] The judgement comes from the first sentence of a Khodasevich obituary that appeared in one of the leading émigré journals. The entire piece, well worth reading, is published in Nabokov's own English translation in Karlinsky and Appel (eds), pp. 83–87.

In short, Khodasevich's poetry can be understood as a cultural barometer of his times. None of his contemporaries doubted his skill as a poet, but readers allowed their broader conceptions of art to influence their appreciation of his achievements. Those who valued continuity (and – though Tynyanov would not have agreed – Pushkin himself was such a poet) admired this verse, while readers who saw art as rupture only grudgingly praised it. Even Tynyanov admitted that Khodasevich had some good poems, though he insisted that they were atypical. The point to be emphasized, however, is that the evaluations of Khodasevich's contemporaries – instructive in terms of understanding the historical context – have lost much of their relevance to readers who come to the work almost a century later. In many ways, Khodasevich's classical precision speaks to us more directly than the extravagant poetry of his contemporaries. His doubts are more appealing than their confidence. Yes, Khodasevich was a 'traditional' poet, but strikingly innovative within the culture that he inherited and inhabited. His approach was in direct opposition to his arch-enemies, the Russian Cubo-Futurists, who advocated – in their manifestos, if not always in their actual practice – 'throwing Pushkin off the steamship of modernity'. In 'God alive!', a polemic against Futurism, Khodasevich celebrates his 'human language', passed down to him 'from generation to generation' and expresses his wish to turn his deathbed moan into an 'articulate ode'. In 'Whyever not the four-foot iamb' he offers a hymn to the iambic tetrameter, 'cherished from before the flood', the most venerable metre of Russian poetry. This magnificent unfinished poem, probably written in 1938, appears to have been his last.

Whether formal qualities should be retained in English poetic translation is an eternal question with no satisfactory and certainly no unequivocal answer. In the case of a poet as form-conscious as Khodasevich, however, the solution is fairly simple: the translator must retain as much as possible of the poet's formal choices. In the translations in this volume, Peter Daniels has taken pains mostly to echo, and sometimes to preserve fully, the rhyme scheme and metre of the original. These are, after all, not simply an adornment to the message, but an integral part of it. In purely metrical terms, Khodasevich's verse stood out in its day as almost wilfully anachronistic.[12]

---

[12] A statistical study of Khodasevich's metrical repertoire shows that his practice 'goes against *every single one* of the distinguishing features' of the Modernist period in Russia. – G.S. Smith, 'The Versification of V.F. Khodasevič', in Thomas Eekman and Dean S. Worth (eds), *Russian Poetics: Proceedings of the International Colloquium at UCLA, September 22–26, 1975* (Slavica, Columbus, Ohio, 1983), p. 388.

It is characteristic that the poem 'The Way of the Seed' is written in iambic hexameter couplets, the Russian equivalent of alexandrines, a form that to a Russian ear has strong eighteenth-century associations and was already considered old-fashioned in Pushkin's day. To use this form in the early twentieth century was to make a statement about tradition just as powerful – and just as overt – as the poem's theme.

If the poetic silence of Khodasevich's last years reflected his forebodings about the survival of his own voice and Russian culture generally, then Peter Daniels' translations, along with the original texts, give us the opportunity to respond to these doubts optimistically. In a new century, Khodasevich speaks to us with a surprising immediacy. It is time to recognize his rightful place in Russian poetry.

# Translator's Preface

VLADISLAV FELITSIANOVICH KHODASEVICH was a modernist, but with a classical temperament. Deeply knowledgeable about Pushkin, he planned a book on him, but only wrote part; he did write a full-length book on Pushkin's predecessor Derzhavin. In form he was conservative, not an experimenter like Tsvetayeva. David Bethea, in his life and work of Khodasevich, compares him for Western readers to Laforgue, Hardy and Auden, calling him 'a transitional figure who stands to the modern Russian lyric tradition as does Auden, *mutatis mutandis*, to that of England and America'. Being younger than Blok and the other Symbolists, Khodasevich rejected their methods and developed his own style with parallels to Western modernism, rooting feelings and thoughts in precise factual description developing the kind of unified 'system of images, thoughts, feelings, and sounds' he described in relation to Derzhavin. In his post-Symbolist work he developed his sceptical eye and sardonic tone, his detachment from the Russian mainstream much emphasized by the frustrations of exile. In *Sorrento Photographs,* one of the great Russian longer poems of the twentieth century, he expresses, in a manner both playful and moving, feelings of dissociation as an observer of the Italian scene and of the Russian memories that intrude on it.

As an émigré he was ignored or criticized by the Soviet authorities, and émigré writers were not much noticed in the West at that time. His essay 'Infancy' is quoted by David Bethea: 'I made my appearance in poetry precisely when the most significant of all modern trends [i.e. Symbolism] had begun to exhaust itself, yet the time for something new had still not set in [. . .]. Tsvetayeva [. . .] and I, having emerged from Symbolism, attached ourselves to nothing and to no one, and remained forever solitary, "wild". Literary classifiers and compilers of anthologies don't know where to stick us.'

Tsvetaeyva has become much noticed and translated in the West. Her biography has the drama of an unconventional life in exile, a return to Soviet Russia, and suicide; her work was technically ground-breaking, and so suitable material for the study of modernist poetics, and she has been of absorbing interest for women's studies in recent decades. Khodasevich has not attracted this kind of attention: his exile kept him absent from direct Stalinist oppression, and although culturally he clearly belongs to modernism, his work is self-consciously classical in form. His quieter tragedy ended in a natural death just before World War Two: with his Jewish background he would otherwise inevitably have been sent from Paris to Auschwitz like his widow Olga. His former partner Nina Berberova went to America and eventually taught at Princeton University, which has helped to cultivate the beginnings of Western interest in him. Nabokov looked up to Khodasevich as the 'greatest Russian poet of our time', and the character of Koncheyev in *The Gift* is partly based on him, but this has not led to fame for him in the West. Brodsky admired him; in the Soviet Union his work circulated in samizdat alongside Brodsky's, and the Uzbek writer Hamid Izmailov has told me that their authorship even became confused. His reputation is now fully reestablished in Russia.

## Life

Khodasevich was born in Moscow in 1886, the youngest of six. His parents were Lithuanian Poles from Vilnius (like the family of Czesław Miłosz). His father was an artist who turned to photography and became Moscow's first Kodak dealer (see 'The Dactyls'). His maternal grandparents were Jewish; his grandfather Yakov Branfman had written about oppression of poor Jews by rich ones, which left him alienated from the Jewish community and he converted. Vladislav's mother introduced him at an early age to the poetry of Mickiewicz. The poem 'Not my mother. . .' is about his Russian wet nurse, who gave him 'the excruciating right' both to love and to curse the 'thundering power' of Russia. Although he was Russified by his education he felt he had to claim that right: his Polish heritage gave him a somewhat oblique perspective on Russia and its poetry, despite his deep knowledge and love of it (see 'I was born in Moscow. . .').

He began publishing poetry with the collection *Molodost'* (Youth) in 1908, having already identified himself as a poet at school. A schoolfellow of Valery Bryusov's younger brother, he worked on Symbolist literary periodicals for a number of years, but, significantly younger than writers like Blok and Bely, he eventually felt the need to develop a post-Symbolist poetry.

He had married his cousin Marina Ryndina in 1905, but in 1911 he went to Venice, pursuing an affair with Yevgenia (Zhenya) Muratova. She was the wife of his friend Pavel Muratov, an art historian who was an excellent guide to the sights, and especially Veronese's paintings which inspired Khodasevich deeply. The affair ended (see 'Nothing more lovely. . .'), but this trip introduced a new perspective beyond the kind of vague, attitudinizing poetry he had been writing. In the autumn of that year his mother died in a horrific street accident, and his grieving father died soon after; he also met Anna Chulkova (Anyuta) who became his second wife. These biographical elements contributed to the maturing of his poetry.

Khodasevich was never in good health. As a baby he only just survived and was kept on special diets; he was faddy about food, and many of his later health troubles were perhaps due to scurvy. He was aware of death as always very close, from personal experience, which he describes in the poem 'An Episode'. In 1916 tuberculosis of the spine developed from a back injury; in March that year his closest friend Muni (Samuil Kissin) committed suicide, and Khodasevich blamed himself for not being there to help him (see notes to 'Look for Me').

In 1917 Khodasevich began to prepare Russian translations of the new Hebrew poets writing in Russia, eventually published as an anthology in 1922. He knew no Hebrew but worked from literal versions, with transliterations of the original for the sound. Khodasevich maintained an interest in his own Jewish heritage as well as the Polish. At this time he was also developing a deep friendship with the Jewish scholar Mikhail Gershenzon, an expert on Pushkin.

He lived in Moscow: his poem '2nd November' gives a vivid description of the aftermath of the October Revolution, and is one of seven poems in blank verse he wrote between 1918 and 1920. Blank verse is untypical in Russian poetry, but had been used by Pushkin; Khodasevich's poem 'The House' clearly refers to Pushkin's 'Again I visited. . .' and the freedom of blank verse suggests an impulse to something approaching modernist free verse, but looking back to Pushkin as a model. His blank verse is much more regularly iambic than the typical English pentameter with its substituted feet.

In 1920, encouraged by Gorky, Khodasevich moved to Petrograd (Petersburg) and became a resident of Dom Iskusstv (House of the Arts), which Gorky had helped to establish for a group of writers and translators led by Korney Chukovsky (see 'To the Visitor' and 'Ballad of the Heavy Lyre'). This period was both creative and frustrating, at a time of upheaval that saw the death of Blok and the execution of Gumilyov. Gorky left the country, and publishing began to be increasingly under Soviet state control: Khodasevich undertook various kinds of official literary work. In early 1922 he and Nina Berberova began their relationship (see notes to 'I play at cards. . .').

He left Russia in 1922 with Nina – they seem never to have formally married – and went first to Berlin, like many Russians. They spent much of the first few years of their exile in the company of Gorky, at

Saarow, a spa on a lake near Berlin where Gorky had a dacha, and in Prague, Marienbad, Venice and Sorrento. A brief stay in Belfast, where Nina evidently had a cousin, was not a success. In 1925 they settled in Paris, working in the exasperating Russian émigré literary world, where Khodasevich wrote less and less poetry. He and Nina separated in 1932 but remained on good terms, and he married Olga Margolina in 1933. He died of liver cancer in June 1939.

### My translations of Khodasevich

Khodasevich came to my attention when I read Michael Wachtel's *The Development of Russian Verse* to prepare for some work on translations from Russian in 2009. 'The Dactyls' struck me as surprisingly contemporary in the way it showed a man looking at his father (and no doubt echoing how I would like to write about my own father). I felt this poem and others such as 'The Monkey' had an affinity with the kind of poetic tradition I associate with Robert Frost and Elizabeth Bishop; what the late Michael Donaghy (also a poet of this kind) called, in his essay 'The Exile's Accent', 'those poets whose craft is driven not by a desire to express a confidently anchored "natural" self, but by a need to create a self through the work'. Reading further in his poetry, I enjoyed Khodasevich's combination of passion and ironic outlook, and sympathized with his sense of being a misfit – too late for Symbolism and tired of Decadence, unimpressed by Futurism and other attempts to break the mould of his beloved Pushkin. Once he had developed from being an epigone of the Symbolists, he acquired a strong personal identity, his formal conservatism containing a precisely observed modernist content and highly individual lyric voice. I found in him some of what Donaghy called in Auden, Bishop and James Merrill 'that arch elegance, that courageous affectation'. I felt excited and moved by the delayed flowering of his vocation as a poet from about 1916, until he practically abandoned it after his final settlement in Paris. Marooned in exile, he did not have to face the terrors of Stalin's regime unlike Mandelshtam, Akhmatova, Pasternak and Tsvetayeva, but that does not make him a lesser poet; it does make him less visible. I can admit to feeling that perhaps, for the English-speaking world, I had to be the stranger with the spade in his poem 'Gold', who unearths the gold coin of his soul, 'a tiny sun' buried with him as his passport to the future life.

Coming to him as a poet with a working knowledge of Russian, I have intended always to provide a satisfactory poem in English that conveys as much as possible of Khodasevich's intended meaning.

These are attempts at translated poems, rather than free versions or imitations, but I have been more free with meanings in some places where it was necessary to make the English work. While his voice is modern, he does use many words marked *obs.* or *poet.* in the dictionary: mostly I have not tried to reproduce this except by seeking an appropriate tone and register in modern English. I have depended on my mentor Masha Karp to ensure that I have captured the subtleties as much as I could.

I am not a 'new formalist' poet, although my use of rhyme in these translations might suggest that. In some of my early translations I was less concerned with rhyme, and was naturally drawn to the blank verse poems, but 'Ballad of the Heavy Lyre' and 'The Stars' self-evidently needed rhyme if they were to work at all. Sharpening my technique on those two helped me after that to come closer to satisfying the Russian love of rhyme, in the search for an appropriate verse music to echo the original, though in many poems I have rhymed only alternate lines rather than attempt the full pattern, and I have not tried the Russian alternation of feminine and masculine rhymes.

From other people's readings of my own poems as well as these translations, it seems to me that verse reading in English is remarkably subjective, with no common approach to metre and how it works. I can only say that all the metre in this book works for me when read aloud. In case of difficulty I suggest reading it again with a different emphasis, as the availability of varying stress in English as part of intonation for meaning can cause confusion. I believe that the element of timing in poetry is seriously underestimated, and this especially applies to ballad metre and similar forms: in a poem like 'In Petrovsky Park' there is a natural final beat at the end of the line equivalent to a rest in music, but sometimes there is a need to fill it with a syllable, and either of these may 'look' wrong. In more formal metres the texture of words can also naturally create a rubato within the overall timing of the line, and I find this applies to some quatrains that retain a kind of folk-memory of the ballad. I am glad to see that in Glyn Maxwell's recent book *On Poetry*\* he emphasizes how essential time is in verse. I do find the application of traditional prosodic feet helpful, but Maxwell prefers to base it all on time: 'In terms of musical notation, one should think of the stresses – the beats, the metre – as the *bars*, not as the notes, not as the crotchets or minims or breves' (*On Poetry*, p. 86). The reader completes the poem by taking it from the page and putting it into real time: 'Poets are voices upon time.

---

\*Oberon Masters, London, 2012.

What makes poetry so giddyingly different from other forms is how naturally and plainly its reader can inhabit that voice' (*On Poetry*, p. 14).

Khodasevich had his own strong views on the workings of poetry, notably the inextricability of form and content. He has been and will continue to be a fascinating companion, and I am very grateful to have encountered him.

*Peter Daniels*
*Stoke Newington, London*
*March 2013*

*Order of the poems*

The poems in this book appear not in chronological order of composition but following the order Khodasevich gave them in his own carefully arranged publications. Although this is only a selection, much of the significance remains, as for instance with 'A Variation', its title specifically intended to follow 'An Episode', or in the tonal contrast between the expansive, humorous 'The Music' juxtaposed with the tight, guilt-ridden 'Lady's washed her hands so long'. Two unpublished poems, 'The Dove' and 'I know the coffin-craftsman's working' (pp. 86–87), are best understood as an appendix to *The Way of the Seed*, since they relate closely to '2nd November'. The other uncollected and unpublished poems selected here date from Khodasevich's period in exile and are presented chronologically after *European Night*, the last collection to appear in his lifetime, which was published as part of his 1927 Paris retrospective volume.

# Translator's Acknowledgements

My thanks are due to the Stephen Spender Foundation and the Hawthornden Trust for a fellowship at Hawthornden Castle in November 2009 with the specific intention to spend time on translating poetry, and to Graham Fawcett for putting my name forward for the fellowship. Graham's translation workshops at the Poetry School brought me back to poetry after several years, while opening up new avenues and especially this one. The excellent books of Michael Wachtel and David Bethea were indispensable, and trips from Hawthornden to the National Library of Scotland and the Scottish Poetry Library in Edinburgh helped me get started.

I have received expert advice on idioms and cultural references from Svetlana Balashova and her daughter Delia Meylanova; Robert Chandler; Irina Mashinski; and most of all Masha Karp, who has become my regular mentor and friend. For the project of making a collection of English poems from Khodasevich's Russian, early encouragement came from Mimi Khalvati, and from Michael Schmidt's enthusiasm to publish some of my first attempts in *PN Review*. My publisher Antony Wood has been exemplary.

The translations in this book, in some cases earlier versions, have first appeared in magazines as follows:

*The Bow-Wow Shop*: 'From the Window', 'Petersburg', 'The babble of spring. . .', 'While your soul bursts out in youth'.
*Cardinal Points*: 'Nights', 'The House', 'The Dove', 'The Music', 'Not my mother. . .', 'Lady's washed her hands so long', 'To the Visitor', 'Giselle', 'The Stopper', 'The Swallows', 'Step over, leap across', 'Twilight', 'Onto the tarnished spires', 'God alive! I'm not beyond coherence', 'Through the consoling April sun'.
*The Dark Horse*: 'In Petrovsky Park'.
*The Long Poem Magazine*: '2nd November'.
*Modern Poetry in Translation*: 'An Encounter', 'Ballad of the One-Armed Man', 'Whyever not the four-foot iamb'.
*PN Review*: 'Gold', 'The Monkey', 'Ballad of the Heavy Lyre', 'The Stars'.
*Poetry Review*: 'The Dactyls'.

*Texts*

In my reading of Khodasevich I have used mostly *Sobraniye sochineniy*, ed. John Malmstad and Robert Hughes, 2 vols (poetry is vol. 1), Ardis, Ann Arbor, 1983; rev. ed. Moscow, 2009, planned as an eight-volume collected works. Before obtaining my own copy of Malmstad and Hughes I used post-Soviet pocket selections: *Po Bul'varam* (Tsentr-100, Moscow, 1996) and *Lirika* (Kharvest, Minsk, 1999). I have also consulted Yuri Kolker's two-volume edition, compiled under difficult circumstances in the Soviet Union and published in Paris by La Presse Libre, 1983; and, on questions of dating poems, *Stikhotvoreniya*, ed. N.A. Bogomolov and D.B. Volchek, in the Biblioteka Poeta series, 3rd ed., Sovetskiy Pisatel', Leningrad, 1989. Khodasevich's works are available online at: http://az.lib.ru/h/hodasewich_w_f/

Dimitri Obolensky's *Penguin Russian Poets* (1962; reissued as *The Heritage of Russian Verse*, Indiana University Press, 1976) and Donald Rayfield et al., *The Garnett Book of Russian Verse* (London, 2000), contain four and eleven poems respectively, with literal prose translations. The originals of seventeen poems appeared in the parallel text edition *Modern Russian Poetry*, eds Vladimir Markov and Merrill Sparks (MacGibbon and Kee, London, 1966).

P.D.

*Publisher's acknowledgement*

The publisher gratefully acknowledges the help of Professor Donald Rayfield in putting the Cyrillic texts into electronic form for printing.

# Some Further Reading

Michael Basker, 'The Trauma of Exile: An Extended Analysis of Khodasevich's "Sorrentinskie Fotografii"', *Toronto Slavic Quarterly*, No. 33, Summer 2010, pp. 5–165. A thorough study of the complexities of 'Sorrento Photographs' is available at http://www.utoronto.ca/tsq/33/tsq_33_basker.pdf

Nina Berberova, *The Italics are Mine*, trans. Philippe Radley, Chatto and Windus, London, 1991

David Bethea, *Khodasevich: His life and art*, Princeton University Press, 1983. Biography and detailed consideration of his poems; prepared with the cooperation of Nina Berberova

Simon Karlinsky and Alfred Appel, eds, *The Bitter Air of Exile: Russian writers in the West 1922–1972*, rev. ed., University of California Press, Berkeley, 1977. Contains essays on Khodasevich by Robert Hughes and Vladimir Nabokov, as well as Nabokov's translations of three poems and an essay by Khodasevich, 'Tolstoy's Departure'

Carl R. Proffer and Joseph Brodsky, eds, *Modern Russian Poets on Poetry*, Ardis, Ann Arbor, 1974. Includes Khodasevich's 1921 lecture on Pushkin, 'The Shaken Tripod'

Michael Wachtel, *The Development of Russian Verse: Metre and its meanings*, Cambridge University Press, Cambridge, 1999

*Previous verse translations of Khodasevich's poems in English*

The most eminent translators have been Vladimir Nabokov (three poems and a fragment in *Verses and Versions*, Harcourt, San Diego, CA, 2008; two also appear in *Russian Poets*, Alfred A. Knopf, New York and Everyman, London, 2009); Charles Tomlinson (four poems in *Translations*, Oxford University Press, 1983); and Michael Frayn (ten poems in *Twentieth-Century Russian Poetry*, Fourth Estate, London and Bantam Doubleday, New York, 1993). Daniel Weissbort has translated four poems, alongside two by Mary Jane White and one by John Glad, in *Twentieth-Century Russian Poetry* (University of Iowa Press, Iowa City, 1992).

The website www.russianpoetry.net hosted at Northwestern University, Evanston, IL, contains eight poems in parallel text, translated by Andrew Wachtel, Tatiana Tulchinsky and Gwenan Wilbur, unrhymed in the interests of 'staying close enough to the original to allow its idiosyncrasies to come through in translation'.

Other translations are as follows: Alexander Landman published thirty-six poems in *Russian Literature Triquarterly* (Winter 1974) of which twelve also appeared in Victor Terras, *Poetry of the Silver Age* (Dresden, 1998), along with seven by Terras; Markov and Sparks have verse translations of their seventeen poems (see Translator's Acknowledgements –*Texts*); three by David Brummell appear in *Modern Poetry in Translation* (Winter 1996).

# SELECTED POEMS

# НОЧИ

*Сергею Кречетову*

Чуть воют псы сторожевые.
Сегодня там же, где вчера,
Кочевий скудных дети злые,
Мы руки греем у костра.

И дико смотрит исподлобья
Пустых ночей глухая сонь.
В дыму рубиновые хлопья,
Свистя, гремя, кружит огонь.

Молчит пустыня. В даль без звука
Колючий ветер гонит прах, –
И наших песен злая скука
Язвя, кривится на губах. . .

Чуть воют псы сторожевые.

*7 мая 1907*
*Лидино*

# Nights

*for Sergey Krechetov*

A thin howl from the dogs on guard.
Another night, still where we were:
a camp of no-good vagabond children,
warming our hands beside the fire.

A sullen look beneath the brows
from nights of nothing wrapped in sleep.
Ruby floaters whirl in smoke
from flames that whistle and crack the whip.

The waste says nothing. Silently
the wind drives onward, barbed with dust;
the dreary evil of our singing
scratches our lips and makes them twist. . .

A thin howl from the dogs on guard.

*7 May 1907*
*Lidino*

* * *

Жеманницы былых годов,
Читательницы Ричардсона!
Я посетил ваш ветхий кров,
Взглянул с высокого балкона

На дальние луга, на лес,
И сладко было мне сознанье,
Что мир ваш навсегда исчез
И с ним его очарованье.

Что больше нет в саду цветов,
В гостиной – нот на клавесине,
И вечных вздохов стариков
О матушке-Екатерине.

Рукой не прикоснулся я
К томам библиотеки пыльной,
Но радостен был для меня
Их запах, затхлый и могильный.

Я думал: в грустном сем краю
Уже полвека всё пустует.
О, пусть отныне жизнь мою
Одно грядущее волнует!

Блажен, кто средь разбитых урн,
На невозделанной куртине,
Прославит твой полет, Сатурн,
Сквозь многозвездные пустыни!

*Конец 1912*

* * *

Precious ladies long ago,
Richardson-reading company;
I visited your ancient home,
glanced from the lofty balcony

at far-off meadowlands and woods,
and sweetly came the realization:
all your world has disappeared
and gone is all its fascination.

Gardens with no flowers now,
a harpsichord that no one plays;
no more the old men's endless sighs
for darling Empress Catherine's days.

I did not run my fingers down
the books that stood in serried rows,
and yet their mouldy graveyard smell
I found congenial to my nose.

I thought how fifty years have left
this place deserted, void and glum.
O may my life be troubled now
entirely by the things to come!

I walk in bliss through flowerbeds
of broken urns, and glorify
thy flight, O Saturn, over us
along the empty starry sky.

*End of 1912*

## ВЕЧЕР

Красный Марс восходит над агавой,
Но прекрасней светят нам они –
Генуи, в былые дни лукавой,
Мирные, торговые огни.

Меркнут гор прибрежные отроги,
Пахнет пылью, морем и вином.
Запоздалый ослик на дороге
Торопливо плещет бубенцом. . .

Не в такой ли час, когда ночные
Небеса синели надо всем,
На таком же ослике Мария
Покидала тесный Вифлеем?

Топотали частые копыта,
Отставал Иосиф, весь в пыли. . .
Что еврейке бедной до Египта,
До чужих овец, чужой земли?

Плачет мать. Дитя под черной тальмой
Сонными губами ищет грудь,
А вдали, вдали звезда над пальмой
Беглецам указывает путь.

*Весна 1913*

# Evening

The red of Mars rises above the agave,
but prettier the lights that shine to us
where Genoa, cunning city of the old days,
twinkles with its peaceful busyness.

Darkness falls on hilly coastal headlands,
dust and sea and wine give out their smells.
Late on the road, a hurried little donkey
trots with a splashing sound of harness bells.

Was it not such a time, as evening skies
deepened their blueness over everything,
when such a donkey would have carried Mary,
leaving the crowded town of Bethlehem?

Rapid hooftaps clattering away;
the dust against him, Joseph falls behind. . .
Poor Jewish girl, and what has she to do
with Egypt's foreign sheep, its foreign ground?

The mother weeps; inside her black burnous
her baby seeks the breast with drowsy mouth
while far, far overhead, above a palm,
the star will show the fugitives a path.

*Spring 1913*

## ПУТЕМ ЗЕРНА

Проходит сеятель по ровным бороздам.
Отец его и дед по тем же шли путям.

Сверкает золотом в его руке зерно,
Но в землю черную оно упасть должно.

И там, где червь слепой прокладывает ход,
Оно в заветный срок умрет и прорастет.

Так и душа моя идет путем зерна:
Сойдя во мрак, умрет – и оживет она.

И ты, моя страна, и ты, ее народ,
Умрешь и оживешь, пройдя сквозь этот год, –

Затем, что мудрость нам единая дана:
Всему живущему идти путем зерна.

*23 декабря 1917*

# The Way of the Seed

Here's the sower walking along the even rows:
his father, and father's father, went the way he goes.

Here's the seedcorn sparkling golden in his hand,
only to fall into the blackness of the land.

And where the worm is blindly tunnelling a path,
a seed will find its moment for dying, and for growth.

The path my soul will take is like the way of the grain:
it goes down to the dark – to die, and live again.

And you my native country, and her people, you
will perish and survive, after this year is through –

because this single wisdom is given us to obey:
every thing that lives shall go the seedcorn's way.

*23 December 1917*

# АКРОБАТ

*Надпись к силуэту*

От крыши до крыши протянут канат.
Легко и спокойно идет акробат.

В руках его – палка, он весь – как весы,
А зрители снизу задрали носы.

Толкаются, шепчут: «Сейчас упадет!» –
И каждый чего-то взволнованно ждет.

Направо – старушка глядит из окна,
Налево – гуляка с бокалом вина.

Но небо прозрачно, и прочен канат.
Легко и спокойно идет акробат.

А если, сорвавшись, фигляр упадет
И, охнув, закрестится лживый народ, –

Поэт, проходи с безучастным лицом:
Ты сам не таким ли живешь ремеслом?

*1913, 1921*

# The Acrobat

*Caption for a silhouette*

A cable is stretching from rooftop to roof.
The acrobat crosses it, cool and aloof.

He's turned into scales, adjusting his cane
to balance above the spectators, who crane.

They jostle and whisper, 'He's going to fall!'
They're nervous, expecting the end of it all.

At a window, a crone is inspecting the scene;
while a reveller opposite glugs at his wine.

But the sky is transparent, the cable is firm.
The acrobat crosses it, easy and calm.

If the showman should slip and come tumbling down,
and, crossing themselves, they all heartlessly groan –

poet, pass by with an unconcerned face:
for doesn't your craft put you there in his place?

*1913, 1921*

## ПРО СЕБЯ

### 1

Нет, есть во мне прекрасное, но стыдно
Его назвать перед самим собой,
Перед людьми ж – подавно: с их обидной
Душа не примирится похвалой.

И вот – живу, чудесный образ мой
Скрыв под личиной низкой и ехидной...
Взгляни, мой друг: по травке золотой
Ползет паук с отметкой крестовидной.

Пред ним ребенок спрячется за мать,
И ты сама спешишь его согнать
Рукой брезгливой с шейки розоватой.

И он бежит от гнева твоего,
Стыдясь себя, не ведая того,
Что значит знак его спины мохнатой.

*30 ноября 1918*

### 2

Нет, ты не прав, я не собой пленен.
Что доброго в наемнике усталом?
Своим чудесным, божеским началом,
Смотря в себя, я сладко потрясен.

Когда в стихах, в отображенье малом,
Мне подлинный мой образ обнажен, –
Все кажется, что я стою, склонен,
В вечерний час над водяным зерцалом,

И чтоб мою к себе приблизить высь,
Гляжу я в глубь, где звезды занялись.
Упав туда, спокойно угасает

Нечистый взор моих земных очей,
Но пламенно оттуда проступает
Венок из звезд над головой моей.

*17 января 1919*

# On Himself

### 1

No, in my self there's beauty, but I won't
allow myself to call it that, for shame.
So much the more my soul is jarred in front
of people's tiresome praising of my name.

I'm here, alive: my holy icon face
hidden beneath a mask, low and malign.
My friend, look: on this golden stalk of grass,
a crawling spider, with a cross-shaped sign.

A child has seen him, hides in mother's skirt;
your squeamish hand brushes him off like dirt
when he has landed on your pinkish neck.

And now he's scuttling from your angry hand
in shame, but has no way to understand
the mark he carries on his hairy back.

*30 November 1918*

### 2

No, I'm not a narcissist – what good
could be this worn-out vehicle I've hired?
It's when I recognize the spark of God,
the miracle inside, I'm sweetly stirred.

When to myself in verse I represent
in miniature my bare authentic face
it always seems as if I'm standing bent
above a watery twilit looking-glass.

And, so that I can rise towards the height,
I scan the depths, where stars come into light.
The unclean vision of my earthly eyes,

once it has dropped there, gently disappears,
but out of it a fiery wreath will rise,
to garland my reflected head with stars.

*17 January 1919*

## СНЫ

Так! наконец-то мы в своих владеньях!
Одежду – на пол, тело – на кровать.
Ступай, душа, в безбрежных сновиденьях
 Томиться и страдать!

Дорогой снов, мучительных и смутных,
Бреди, бреди, несовершенный дух.
О, как еще ты в проблесках минутных
 И слеп, и глух!

Еще томясь в моем бессильном теле,
Сквозь грубый слой земного бытия
Учись дышать и жить в ином пределе,
 Где ты – не я;

Где, отрешен от помысла земного,
Свободен ты. . . Когда ж в тоске проснусь,
Соединимся мы с тобою снова
 В нерадостный союз.

День изо дня, в миг пробужденья трудный,
Припоминаю я *твой* вещий сон,
Смотрю в окно и вижу серый, скудный
 *Мой* небосклон,

Всё тот же двор, и мглистый, и суровый,
И голубей, танцующих на нем. . .
Лишь явно мне, что некий отсвет новый
 Лежит на всем.

*17 декабря 1917*

# Dreams

So! Now at last we have come to our home territories!
Clothes are down on the floor, and body up on the bed.
Step now, my soul, into the boundless dreamscape, to
    languish and suffer!

Down the road of dreams, excruciating, troubled,
keep trudging and trudging, my imperfect spirit.
Even when enlightenment flashes – oh, you are
    so blind, so deaf.

Agonizing still inside my powerless body,
through the rough layer of this earthly being
learn how to breathe and live in this other land where
    you are not me.

Where now released from earthly aspirations
you have been freed. . . Until I wake in sadness
and we are reunited, you and I, again in
    unjoyful union.

Day after day, in that heavy moment of waking
I recollect prophetic dreams of yours, and
look from the window, seeing the grey and meagre
    sky that is mine.

Always the same back yard, foggy and bleak,
and the pigeons that are dancing around in it. . .
Only for me now some kind of new light has
    fallen all around.

*17 December 1917*

## В ПЕТРОВСКОМ ПАРКЕ

Висел он, не качаясь,
На узком ремешке.
Свалившаяся шляпа
Чернела на песке.
В ладонь впивались ногти
На стиснутой руке.

А солнце восходило,
Стремя к полудню бег,
И, перед этим солнцем
Не опуская век,
Был высоко приподнят
На воздух человек.

И зорко, зорко, зорко
Смотрел он на восток.
Внизу столпились люди
В притихнувший кружок.
И был почти невидим
Тот узкий ремешок.

*27 ноября 1916*

# In Petrovsky Park

He hung, but was not swinging,
upon a slender band.
His fallen hat, a spot of black,
was lying on the sand.
His nails had dug into the palms
of each clenched hand.

The sun continued rising,
striving to reach its noon:
and with unblinking eyelids
under that shining sun,
there rose above Petrovsky Park
this elevated man.

And staring, he outstared the east,
so sharp a stare had he;
the people clustered round below
in taciturnity;
the slender band that held him
was very hard to see.

*27 November 1916*

## СМОЛЕНСКИЙ РЫНОК

Смоленский рынок
Перехожу.
Полет снежинок
Слежу, слежу.
При свете дня
Желтеют свечи;
Всё те же встречи
Гнетут меня.
Всё к той же чаше
Припал – и пью. . .
Соседки наши
Несут кутью.
У церкви – синий
Раскрытый гроб,
Ложится иней
На мертвый лоб. . .
О, лёт снежинок,
Остановись!
Преобразись,
Смоленский рынок!

*12–13 декабря 1916*

# Smolensky Market

Smolensky Market
– wandering by
I trace each snowflake
with my eye.
The candlelight
is dulled by day;
the same old way
pulls down my heart.
I bow once more
at the cup I take. . .
the women next door
bring pies for a wake.
Outside the church
a coffin in blue,
a frosty touch
on the dead man's brow. . .
Oh, wafting snowflake
stop your flight!
Transform your life,
Smolensky Market!

*12–13 December 1916*

# ЭПИЗОД

. . .Это было
В одно из утр, унылых, зимних, вьюжных, –
В одно из утр пятнадцатого года.
Изнемогая в той истоме тусклой,
Которая тогда меня томила,
Я в комнате своей сидел один. Во мне,
От плеч и головы, к рукам, к ногам,
Какое-то неясное струенье
Бежало трепетно и непрерывно –
И, выбежав из пальцев, длилось дальше,
Уж *вне* меня. Я сознавал, что нужно
Остановить его, сдержать в себе, – но воля
Меня покинула. . . Бессмысленно смотрел я
На полку книг, на желтые обои,
На маску Пушкина, закрывшую глаза.
Всё цепенело в рыжем свете утра.
За окнами кричали дети. Громыхали
Салазки по горе, но эти звуки
Неслись во мне как будто бы сквозь толщу
Глубоких вод. . .
В пучину погружаясь, водолаз
Так слышит беготню на палубе и крики
Матросов.
И вдруг – как бы толчок, – но мягкий, осторожный, –
И всё опять мне прояснилось, только
В перемещенном виде. Так бывает,
Когда веслом мы сталкиваем лодку
С песка прибрежного; еще нога
Под крепким днищем ясно слышит землю,
И близким кажется зеленый берег
И кучи дров на нем; но вот качнуло нас –
И берег отступает; стала меньше
Та рощица, где мы сейчас бродили;
За рощей встал дымок; а вот – поверх деревьев
Уже видна поляна, и на ней
Краснеет баня.

Самого себя
Увидел я в тот миг, как этот берег;
Увидел вдруг со стороны, как если б

# An Episode

                              . . . It was on
one of those mornings, dreary, wintry, blizzardy –
one of those mornings; it was nineteen-fifteen.
Exhausted in the dull and languid state
that wore me down in those days, I was sitting
up in my room alone. All through me, from
shoulders and head, to hands and feet, some kind
of vague current was running, tremblingly,
uninterruptedly – and when it had run
out of my fingers, it continued flowing
even *outside* myself. I recognized
the need to stop it, keep it in – but the will
had abandoned me. . . Mindlessly I looked
at the shelf of books, at the yellow wallpaper,
at Pushkin's deathmask, and his closed-up eyes.
Everything froze in morning's rusty light.
Beyond the window, children shrieked. Sledges
rumbled on the hillside, but these sounds
came through to me as if across a thickness
of deep waters. . .
The way a diver, plunging to the deep, would hear
the running about on deck and the shouts
of the sailors.
And then – a sudden kind of shove, but soft,
careful – it all came clear again to me,
but seeming shifted round. The way it felt
was how we'll take an oar and push the boat
off the sand of the bank; while the foot still
can sense the ground under the strong hull,
and we still seem to be close to the green bank
and its piles of timber, but we've been swung round
and the bank moves backwards; getting smaller,
that little wood in which we've just been strolling,
the curl of smoke behind it; over the trees
look, you can see the clearing now; and in it
the bath house glowing scarlet.

                              I could see
my own self at that instant, like the bank;

Смотреть немного сверху, слева. Я сидел,
Закинув ногу на ногу, глубоко
Уйдя в диван, с потухшей папиросой
Меж пальцами, совсем худой и бледный.
Глаза открыты были, но какое
В них было выраженье – я не видел.
Того меня, который предо мною
Сидел, – не ощущал я вовсе. Но другому,
Смотревшему как бы бесплотным взором,
Так было хорошо, легко, спокойно.
И человек, сидящий на диване,
Казался мне простым, давнишним другом,
Измученным годами путешествий.
Как будто бы ко мне зашел он в гости,
И, замолчав среди беседы мирной,
Вдруг откачнулся, и вздохнул, и умер.
Лицо разгладилось, и горькая улыбка
С него сошла.
Так видел я себя недолго: вероятно,
И четверти положенного круга
Секундная не обежала стрелка.
И как пред тем не по своей я воле
Покинул эту оболочку – так же
В нее и возвратился вновь. Но только
Свершилось это тягостно, с усильем,
Которое мне вспомнить неприятно.
Мне было трудно, тесно, как змее,
Которую заставили бы снова
Вместиться в сброшенную кожу. . .

Снова

Увидел я перед собою книги,
Услышал голоса. Мне было трудно
Вновь ощущать всё тело, руки, ноги. . .
Так, весла бросив и сойдя на берег,
Мы чувствуем себя вдруг тяжелее.
Струилось вновь во мне изнеможенье,
Как бы от долгой гребли, – а в ушах
Гудел неясный шум, как пленный отзвук
Озерного или морского ветра.

*25–28 января 1918*

could see suddenly, looking as if sideways
a little above, to the left. I sat
one leg across the other, sunk back deep
into the sofa, cigarette burnt out
between my fingers, all of me thin and pale.
Eyes open, yet what kind of expression
there might have been in them – I didn't see.
That me, the one sitting there in front of me,
I didn't feel him at all. But to the other,
observing as if with a disembodied view,
it felt so good, so easy and so peaceful.
And the person sitting on the sofa
seemed to me a simple, old, old friend,
who had been worn out from years of travelling;
as if it happened that he'd called on me
and, falling silent in our peaceful talk,
he turned suddenly, gave a sigh, and died.
His face lost its wrinkles, the bitter smile
was gone from him.
I only briefly saw myself like this:
in fact the second hand had not quite turned
even a quarter circuit of the dial.
And just as, not through my own will, I left
behind this outer wrapping – I went back
inside it, in the same way. But this only
came to be achieved with pain, with effort,
and to recall it now is not a pleasure.
It was a hard squeeze for me, as if
a snake were forced to put itself again
into its thrown-off skin. . .

                   And once again
I could see my books in front of me,
I could hear voices. It was hard, once more
to sense all of my body, hands and feet. . .
The way, oars dropped, landing upon the bank,
we feel that we are getting suddenly heavier.
Exhaustion's current ran through me again,
as if from a long rowing – while my ears
hummed with a vague noise like a captive echo
sent from the wind out on a lake, or sea.

*25–28 January 1918*

# ВАРИАЦИЯ

Вновь эти плечи, эти руки
Погреть я вышел на балкон.
Сижу – но все земные звуки –
Как бы во сне или сквозь сон.

И вдруг, изнеможенья полный,
Плыву: куда – не знаю сам,
Но мир мой ширится, как волны,
По разбежавшимся кругам.

Продлись, ласкательное чудо!
Я во второй вступаю круг
И слушаю, уже оттуда,
Моей качалки мерный стук.

*Август 1919*
*Москва*

# A Variation

Out on the balcony again
to warm my shoulders and my arms.
But when I sit there, all the sounds
on earth come through like sounds in dreams.

At once, I'm filled with lassitude
and float somewhere unknown to me:
but there's my world, in spreading rings
dispersed like ripples on the sea.

Endearing wonder, carry on!
I join the second circle, where
I listen to the distant steady
knocking of my rocking chair.

*August 1919*
*Moscow*

# ЗОЛОТО

Иди, вот уже золото кладем в уста твои, уже
мак и мед кладем тебе в руки. Salve æternum.
*Красиньский*


В рот – золото, а в руки – мак и мед;
Последние дары твоих земных забот.

Но пусть не буду я, как римлянин, сожжен:
Хочу в земле вкусить утробный сон,

Хочу весенним злаком прорасти,
Кружась по древнему, по звездному пути.

В могильном сумраке истлеют мак и мед,
Провалится монета в мертвый рот. . .

Но через много, много темных лет
Пришлец неведомый отроет мой скелет,

И в черном черепе, что заступом разбит,
Тяжелая монета загремит –

И золото сверкнет среди костей,
Как солнце малое, как след души моей.

*7 января 1917*

# Gold

Go: now we place gold in your mouth, and we place
poppy and honey in your hands. Salve aeternum.
KRASIŃSKI

A gold coin in the mouth; hands full of poppy and honey:
these are the final gifts of your earthly business.

And don't let them incinerate me like a Roman:
I want to taste my sleep in the womb of the earth.

I want to rise again as the spring corn,
circle the ancient track that the stars follow.

In the darkening grave, poppy and honey will rot,
the dead man's mouth will swallow the gold coin. . .

But after many many years of darkness
a stranger will come and dig my skeleton up,

and inside the blackening skull that his spade
smashes, the heavy coin will clang –

and the gold will flash in the midst of bones,
a tiny sun, the imprint of my soul.

*7 January 1917*

# ИЩИ МЕНЯ

Ищи меня в сквозном весеннем свете.
Я весь – как взмах неощутимых крыл,
Я звук, я вздох, я зайчик на паркете,
Я легче зайчика: он – вот, он есть, я был.

Но, вечный друг, меж нами нет разлуки!
Услышь, я здесь. Касаются меня
Твои живые, трепетные руки,
Простертые в текучий пламень дня.

Помедли так. Закрой, как бы случайно,
Глаза. Еще одно усилье для меня –
И на концах дрожащих пальцев, тайно,
Быть может, вспыхну кисточкой огня.

*20 декабря 1917 – 3 января 1918*

# Look for Me

Look for me in spring's transparent air.
I flit like vanishing wings, no heavier than
a sound, a breath, a sunray on the floor;
I'm lighter than that ray – it's there: I'm gone.

But we are friends for ever, undivided!
Listen: I'm here. Your hands can feel the way
to reach me with their living touch, extended
trembling into the restless flame of day.

Happen to close your eyelids, while you linger. . .
Make me one final effort, and you might
find at the nerve-ends of each quivering finger
brushes of secret fire as I ignite.

*20 December 1917 – 3 January 1918*

## 2-го НОЯБРЯ

Семь дней и семь ночей Москва металась
В огне, в бреду. Но грубый лекарь щедро
Пускал ей кровь – и, обессилев, к утру
Восьмого дня она очнулась. Люди
Повыползли из каменных подвалов
На улицы. Так, переждав ненастье,
На задний двор, к широкой луже, крысы
Опасливой выходят вереницей
И прочь бегут, когда вблизи на камень
Последняя спадает с крыши капля. . .
К полудню стали собираться кучки.
Глазели на пробоины в домах,
На сбитые верхушки башен; молча
Толпились у дымящихся развалин
И на стенах следы скользнувших пуль
Считали. Длинные хвосты тянулись
У лавок. Проволок обрывки висли
Над улицами. Битое стекло
Хрустело под ногами. Желтым оком
Ноябрьское негреющее солнце
Смотрело вниз, на постаревших женщин
И на мужчин небритых. И не кровью,
Но горькой желчью пахло это утро.
А между тем уж из конца в конец,
От Пресненской заставы до Рогожской
И с Балчуга в Лефортово, брели,
Теснясь на тротуарах, люди. Шли проведать
Родных, знакомых, близких: живы ль, нет ли?
Иные узелки несли под мышкой
С убогой снедью: так в былые годы
На кладбище москвич благочестивый
Ходил на Пасхе – красное яичко
Съесть на могиле брата или кума. . .

К моим друзьям в тот день пошел и я.
Узнал, что живы, целы, дети дома, –
Чего ж еще хотеть? Побрел домой.
По переулкам ветер, гость залетный,

# 2nd November

Seven days and seven nights Moscow was tossing
in fire, in delirium. But the brutal old quack
bled her profusely – and, strength all gone,
the morning of the eighth day, she came to.
People crept out of the stone-built basements
to the streets – as, after sitting out the storms,
faced with a broad puddle in the back yard, rats
emerge cautiously, single file, until
away they run at the very last splash
as it drops from the roof and hits the stone. . .
Towards midday, small groups began to gather.
They stared at the holes blasted in homes,
the knocked-off tops of towers; silently
they crowded round the smoking ruins,
counting up the tracks in the walls made
by glancing bullets. Long queues were trailing
at the shops. Wires hung in shreds
above the streets. Broken shards of glass
crunched underfoot. With a yellow eye
the unwarming sun of November
was looking down, at women who had aged,
and unshaven men. Not blood: a bitter
bile was what that morning smelt of.
And meanwhile, from one end to the other,
Présnenskaya gate to Rogózhskaya,
and Bálchuga to Lefórtovo, people were
shuffling, jostling on pavements, to see about
family, friends, and dear ones: alive or not?
Others carried bundles of meagre food
under their arms: as in olden times when
at Easter the pious Muscovite would walk
to the graveyard – with a little red egg
to eat over the grave of a brother or godfather. . .

I went to see my friends that day as well.
Found they were alive, safe, children home –
what more could I want? I plodded back home.

Гонял сухую пыль, окурки, стружки.
Домов за пять от дома моего,
Сквозь мутное окошко, по привычке
Я заглянул в подвал, где мой знакомый
Живет столяр. Необычайным делом
Он занят был. На верстаке, вверх дном,
Лежал продолговатый, узкий ящик
С покатыми боками. Толстой кистью
Водил столяр по ящику, и доски
Под кистью багровели. Мой приятель
Заканчивал работу: красный гроб.
Я постучал в окно. Он обернулся.
И, шляпу сняв, я поклонился низко
Петру Иванычу, его работе, гробу,
И всей земле, и небу, что в стекле
Лазурью отражалось. И столяр
Мне тоже покивал, пожал плечами
И указал на гроб. И я ушел.

А на дворе у нас, вокруг корзины
С плетеной дверцей, суетились дети,
Крича, толкаясь и тесня друг друга.
Сквозь редкие, поломанные прутья
Виднелись перья белые. Но вот –
Протяжно заскрипев, открылась дверца,
И пара голубей, плеща крылами,
Взвилась и закружилась: выше, выше,
Над тихою Плющихой, над рекой. . .
То падая, то подымаясь, птицы
Ныряли, точно белые ладьи
В дали морской. Вослед им дети
Свистали, хлопали в ладоши. . . Лишь один,
Лет четырех бутуз, в ушастой шапке,
Присел на камень, растопырил руки,
И вверх смотрел, и тихо улыбался.
Но, заглянув ему в глаза, я понял,
Что улыбается он самому себе,
Той непостижной мысли, что родится
Под выпуклым, еще безбровым лбом,
И слушает в себе биенье сердца,
Движенье соков, рост. . . Среди Москвы,
Страдающей, растерзанной и падшей,

The wind on a flying visit through the lanes
was chasing the dust, cigarette butts, shavings.
Five doors down from my own home,
through the cloudy window, out of habit
I glanced into the basement where my friend
the joiner lives. An unusual commission
kept him busy. Upside down on the bench
there lay a narrow elongated box
with sloping sides. He took a thick brush,
guided it over the box, and under the brush
the boards were turning crimson. My friend
was finishing the job: a red-painted coffin.
I knocked on the window. He turned around.
And, taking off my hat, I made a low bow
to Pyótr Iványch, to his work, the coffin,
and to all the earth, and heaven, reflecting
its azure in the window pane. And the joiner
nodded to me, too, shrugged his shoulders
and pointed at the coffin. And then I left.

And outside our house, round a basket
with a little wicker lid, children were bustling,
shrieking, pushing and crowding each other.
Through the sparse and broken weave
white feathers could be seen. But then –
after long slow creaking, the lid opened,
and a pair of doves, beating their wings,
flew up and circled round: higher, higher,
over quiet Plyushchíkha, over the river. . .
Falling then rising again, the birds
were bobbing like white sailing-boats
distant on the sea. After them, the children
whistled, clapped their hands. . . Only one
four-year-old, chubby, in a flap-eared hat,
sat down on a stone, spread out his arms
and looking up above him, quietly smiled.
But as I met his eyes, I understood
his smile was at himself and at that thought,
incomprehensible, now being born
under his bulging, not-yet-eyebrowed forehead;
listening to himself, the beating heart,
the moving fluids, growth. . . In Moscow's heart

Как идол маленький, сидел он, равнодушный,
С бессмысленной, священною улыбкой.
И мальчику я поклонился тоже.

### Дома

Я выпил чаю, разобрал бумаги,
Что на столе скопились за неделю,
И сел работать. Но, впервые в жизни,
Ни «Моцарт и Сальери», ни «Цыганы»
В тот день моей не утолили жажды.

*20 мая – 1 июня 1918*

– suffering, torn apart and violated –
like a little idol sitting placidly
he smiled a meaningless and holy smile.
And to the boy I also made a bow.

                              At home
I gulped some tea, sorted out the papers
that had piled up all week across the table,
and sat down to some work. But for the first
time in my life, not *Mozart and Salieri*
nor *The Gypsies* could alleviate my thirst.

*20 May – 1 June 1918*

## ПОЛДЕНЬ

Как на бульваре тихо, ясно, сонно!
Подхвачен ветром, побежал песок
И на траву плеснул сыпучим гребнем. . .
Теперь мне любо приходить сюда
И долго так сидеть, полузабывшись.
Мне нравится, почти не глядя, слушать
То смех, то плач детей, то по дорожке
За обручем их бег отчетливый. Прекрасно!
Вот шум, такой же вечный и правдивый,
Как шум дождя, прибоя или ветра.

Никто меня не знает. Здесь я просто
Прохожий, обыватель, «господин»
В коричневом пальто и круглой шляпе,
Ничем не замечательный. Вот рядом
Присела барышня с раскрытой книгой. Мальчик
С ведерком и совочком примостился
У самых ног моих. Насупив брови,
Он возится в песке, и я таким огромным
Себе кажусь от этого соседства,
Что вспоминаю,
Как сам я сиживал у львиного столпа
В Венеции. Над этой жизнью малой,
Над головой в картузике зеленом,
Я возвышаюсь, как тяжелый камень,
Многовековый, переживший много
Людей и царств, предательств и геройств.
А мальчик деловито наполняет
Ведерышко песком и, опрокинув, сыплет
Мне на ноги, на башмаки. . . Прекрасно!

И с легким сердцем я припоминаю,
Как жарок был венецианский полдень,
Как надо мною реял недвижимо
Крылатый лев с раскрытой книгой в лапах,
А надо львом, круглясь и розовея,
Бежало облачко. А выше, выше –
Темногустая синь, и в ней катились

# Midday

On the boulevard: how quiet, bright and sleepy!
Caught in the wind, the sand has sprung up,
lapping in a crumbly ridge over the grass.
Nowadays I love to come round here
and sit like this a long time, half-withdrawn.
It pleases me, scarcely glancing up, to listen
to children's laughter, their crying, the clear clop
of their feet on the path, chasing a hoop. Delightful!
This is noise as timeless and as truthful
as noise of raindrops, crashing waves, or wind.

No one knows me. Here I'm simply
a passer-by, a nobody, a 'Mister'
in a brown overcoat and porkpie hat,
nothing remarkable. A young lady has come
to sit alongside, opening her book. A boy
with a bucket and spade has placed himself
right at my feet. Face in a frown,
he romps around in the sand, and I seem
to myself so enormous beside this neighbour
that I recall
how I would sit beside the lion column
in Venice. Above this little life,
above this head in a green cap with a peak,
I tower upwards, like the heavy stone,
many-centuried, that has outlived so many
people and reigns, betrayals and heroics.
And the boy, businesslike, fills up
the tiny bucket with sand and, turning it over,
pours it onto my feet, my shoes. . . Delightful!

So then lightheartedly I recollect
how hot it was in Venice at midday,
how up above my head, motionless, hovered
the winged lion, an open book in his paws,
and up above the lion, rounded and pinkish,
a little cloud flying. And further and further up,

Незримые, но пламенные звезды.
Сейчас они пылают над бульваром,
Над мальчиком и надо мной. Безумно
Лучи их борются с лучами солнца...

                              Ветер
Всё шелестит песчаными волнами,
Листает книгу барышни. И всё, что слышу,
Преображенное каким-то чудом,
Так полновесно западает в сердце,
Что уж ни слов, ни мыслей мне не надо,
И я смотрю как бы обратным взором
В себя.
И так пленительна души живая влага,
Что, как Нарцисс, я с берега земного
Срываюсь и лечу туда, где я один,
В моем родном, первоначальном мире,
Лицом к лицу с собой, потерянным когда-то —
И обретенным вновь... И еле внятно
Мне слышен голос барышни: «Простите,
Который час?»

*19 апреля – 1 мая 1918*

the deep, dense blue, and in it there revolved
the invisible but incandescent stars;
they glow this very minute over the boulevard,
over the boy and over me. Oblivious,
their own rays fight against the rays of the sun...

                                            The wind
still whispers in the waves of sand, leafs
through the young lady's book. And everything
I hear, transformed by something like a miracle,
with such a wholeness falls into my heart
that now I have no need of words or thoughts;
and I can look, as if I'm facing backwards,
into myself.
And a fresh dew upon my soul so charms me
that like Narcissus, from the earthly bank
I break away and leap where I'm alone,
in my own native and original world,
face to face with myself, lost at some time –
and now rediscovered... And I'm almost
unaware of the young lady's voice: 'Excuse me,
what time is it?'

*19 April – 1 May 1918*

# ВСТРЕЧА

В час утренний у Santa Margherita
Я повстречал ее. Она стояла
На мостике, спиной к перилам. Пальцы
На сером камне, точно лепестки,
Легко лежали. Сжатые колени
Под белым платьем проступали слабо. . .
Она ждала. Кого? В шестнадцать лет
Кто грезится прекрасной англичанке
В Венеции? Не знаю – и не должно
Мне знать того. Не для пустых догадок
Ту девушку припомнил я сегодня.
Она стояла, залитая солнцем,
Но мягкие поля панамской шляпы
Касались плеч приподнятых – и тенью
Прохладною лицо покрыли. Синий
И чистый взор лился оттуда, словно
Те воды свежие, что пробегают
По каменному ложу горной речки,
Певучие и быстрые. . . Тогда-то
Увидел я тот взор невыразимый,
Который нам, поэтам, суждено
Увидеть раз и после помнить вечно.
На миг один является пред нами
Он на земле, божественно вселяясь
В случайные лазурные глаза.
Но плещут в нем те пламенные бури,
Но вьются в нем те голубые вихри,
Которые потом звучали мне
В сияньи солнца, в плеске черных го́ндол,
В летучей тени голубя и в красной
Струе вина.

И поздним вечером, когда я шел
К себе домой, о том же мне шептали
Певучие шаги венецианок,
И собственный мой шаг казался звонче,
Стремительней и легче. Ах, куда,
Куда в тот миг мое вспорхнуло сердце,

# An Encounter

Early in the morning at Santa Margherita
I encountered her. She stood
on the little bridge, back to the parapet, fingers
resting on the grey stone as lightly
as petals. In her white dress, vaguely
discernible, her knees were drawn together.
Waiting for someone. Who? Who is the dream
of a sixteen-year-old lovely English girl
in Venice? I don't know – it isn't mine
to know. And not for any pointless conjecture
I recollect that girl again today.
She stood there, immersed in sunshine, but
with the soft brim of her panama touching
her slightly lifted shoulders, and her face
protected by the cooling shade. Deep blue
and pure, her gaze flowed out from there,
like streams of water freshly running through
the stony channel of a mountain rivulet,
melodious and swift. . . In that moment
I could glimpse that look, the inexpressible
it is our destiny as poets once
to catch, and to remember ever after.
It shows itself, a single flash before us,
godlike on earth, coming down at random
to occupy some eyes of lapis lazuli.
But they were brimming with those flaming storms,
twisting inside them were those sky-blue whirlwinds,
which reverberated then for me
in sunshine, in the splash of the black gondolas,
the fleeting shadows of pigeons, and the red
flow of the wine.

And later in the evening, when I walked back
home, I was hearing whispers of the same
from the tuneful stepping of Venetian women,
and I felt my own steps more ringingly,
impetuously, lightly. Ah, but where,

Когда тяжелый ключ с пружинным звоном
Я повернул в замке? И отчего,
Переступив порог сеней холодных,
Я в темноте у каменной цистерны
Стоял так долго? Ощупью взбираясь
По лестнице, влюбленностью назвал я
Свое волненье. Но теперь я знаю,
Что крепкого вина в тот день вкусил я –
И чувствовал еще в своих устах
Его минутный вкус. А вечный хмель
Пришел потом.

*13 мая 1918*

where in that second did it fly away, my heart,
when the heavy key made a springy sound as
I turned it in the lock? And when I'd stepped
across the threshold of the chilly hallway,
why stand in the shade of the stone cistern
quietly, for so long? Groping my way up
the staircase, being in love is what I called
this agitation. Now I realize
I had tasted strong wine that day –
and I was still feeling on my lips
that momentary taste. The eternal drunkenness
came afterwards.

*13 May 1918*

## ОБЕЗЬЯНА

Была жара. Леса горели. Нудно
Тянулось время. На соседней даче
Кричал петух. Я вышел за калитку.
Там, прислонясь к забору, на скамейке
Дремал бродячий серб, худой и черный.
Серебряный тяжелый крест висел
На груди полуголой. Капли пота
По ней катились. Выше, на заборе,
Сидела обезьяна в красной юбке
И пыльные листы сирени
Жевала жадно. Кожаный ошейник,
Оттянутый назад тяжелой цепью,
Давил ей горло. Серб, меня заслышав,
Очнулся, вытер пот и попросил, чтоб дал я
Воды ему. Но чуть ее пригубив, –
Не холодна ли, – блюдце на скамейку
Поставил он, и тотчас обезьяна,
Макая пальцы в воду, ухватила
Двумя руками блюдце.
Она пила, на четвереньках стоя,
Локтями опираясь на скамью.
Досок почти касался подбородок,
Над теменем лысеющим спина
Высоко выгибалась. Так, должно быть,
Стоял когда-то Дарий, припадая
К дорожной луже, в день, когда бежал он
Пред мощною фалангой Александра.
Всю воду выпив, обезьяна блюдце
Долой смахнула со скамьи, привстала
И – этот миг забуду ли когда? –
Мне черную, мозолистую руку,
Еще прохладную от влаги, протянула. . .
Я руки жал красавицам, поэтам,
Вождям народа – ни одна рука
Такого благородства очертаний
Не заключала! Ни одна рука
Моей руки так братски не коснулась!
И, видит Бог, никто в мои глаза
Не заглянул так мудро и глубоко,

# The Monkey

It was hot. Forests were burning. Time
tediously dragging. At the neighbouring dacha
the cockerel crowed. I went out past the gate.
There, propped against the fence, on the bench,
a vagrant was dozing, a Serb, thin and dark.
A cross of heavy silver hung on his
half-naked chest. Drops of sweat
were rolling down him. Up on the fence
a monkey in a red skirt was sitting
greedily chewing the leaves
of the dusty lilacs. Her leather collar
was pulled back by a heavy chain,
catching her throat. The Serb, hearing me,
woke up, wiped off his sweat and asked me
to give him some water. But he barely sipped –
how cold was it? – put a dish on the bench
and at once the monkey, dipping
a finger in the water, seized
the dish in both her hands.
She drank, crouched on all fours,
her elbows leaning on the bench.
Her chin nearly touched the planks,
her backbone arched high above her dark
and balding head. It was the position
Darius must once have taken, bending
at a puddle in the road the day he fled
in front of Alexander's mighty phalanx.
When she had drunk it all, the monkey
swept the dish from the bench, stood up
and – when could I ever forget this moment? –
offered me her black and calloused hand,
still cool from the water, extending it. . .
I have shaken hands with beauties, poets,
leaders of nations – not one hand displayed
a line of such nobility! Not one hand
has ever touched my hand so like a brother's!
God is my witness, no one has looked at me

Воистину – до дна души моей.
Глубокой древности сладчайшие преданья
Тот нищий зверь мне в сердце оживил,
И в этот миг мне жизнь явилась полной,
И мнилось – хор светил и волн морских,
Ветров и сфер мне музыкой органной
Ворвался в уши, загремел, как прежде,
В иные, незапамятные дни.

И серб ушел, постукивая в бубен.
Присев ему на левое плечо,
Покачивалась мерно обезьяна,
Как на слоне индийский магараджа.
Огромное малиновое солнце,
Лишенное лучей,
В опаловом дыму висело. Изливался
Безгромный зной на чахлую пшеницу.

В тот день была объявлена война.

*7 июня 1918, 20 февраля 1919*

so wisely and so deeply in the eye,
indeed into the bottom of my soul.
This animal, destitute, called up in my heart
the sweetness of a deep and ancient legend.
Life in that instant seemed to me complete;
a choir of sea-waves, winds and spheres
was shining and was bursting in my ear
with organ music, thundering, as once
it did in other, immemorial days.

Then the Serb got up, patted a tambourine.
Taking up her seat on his left shoulder
with measured rocking, the monkey rode
like a maharajah on an elephant.
The enormous crimson sun
stripped of its rays
hung in the opalescent smoke. A sultry
thunderlessness covered the feeble wheat.

That was the day of the declaration of war.

*7 June 1918, 20 February 1919*

# ДОМ

Здесь домик был. Недавно разобрали
Верх на дрова. Лишь каменного низа
Остался грубый остов. Отдыхать
Сюда по вечерам хожу я часто. Небо
И дворика зеленые деревья
Так молодо встают из-за развалин,
И ясно так рисуются пролеты
Широких окон. Рухнувшая балка
Похожа на колонну. Затхлый холод
Идет от груды мусора и щебня,
Засыпавшего комнаты, где прежде
Гнездились люди. . .
Где ссорились, мирились, где в чулке
Замызганные деньги припасались
Про черный день; где в духоте и мраке
Супруги обнимались; где потели
В жару больные; где рождались люди
И умирали скрытно, – всё теперь
Прохожему открыто. О, блажен,
Чья вольная нога ступает бодро
На этот прах, чей посох равнодушный
В покинутые стены ударяет!
Чертоги ли великого Рамсеса,
Поденщика ль безвестного лачуга –
Для странника равны они: всё той же
Он песенкою времени утешен;
Ряды ль колонн торжественных, иль дыры
Дверей вчерашних – путника всё так же
Из пустоты одной ведут они в другую
Такую же. . .
                    Вот лестница с узором
Поломанных перил уходит в небо,
И, обрываясь, верхняя площадка
Мне кажется трибуною высокой.
Но нет на ней оратора. – А в небе
Уже горит вечерняя звезда,
Водительница гордого раздумья.

\*

# The House

There was a house here. They recently dismantled
the upstairs for firewood, leaving just the rough
lower stonework structure. I go there
often of an evening to relax. The open sky
and green trees in the little courtyard
rise up so fresh from all that's fallen,
and there's the clear outline of the wide
window-frames. A tumbled beam resembles
a column. A musty chill is coming
from the piles of rubble and debris
filling up the rooms, where there was once
a nest of people. . .
Where they quarrelled, they reconciled, they
stored up greasy money in a stocking
for a rainy day; where in the stuffy dark
couples embraced; where they sweated
in a fever's heat; where people were born
and died in private – all of it now
open to the passer-by. O, blessed is he
whose untrammelled foot treads cheerfully
on this dust, and whose indifferent staff
can knock against the abandoned walls!
The royal palace of great Rameses
or an unknown labourer's shack, they're
equal to the wanderer, taking the same
comfort in the song of passing time; whether
ceremonious ranks of columns, or gaps
from yesterday's doors, much the same
they lead the traveller from one emptiness
into another. . .
           With a pattern of broken banisters
the stairs are walking up into the sky,
and where the landing has been interrupted
seems to me like an elevated podium.
But there's no orator. And in the sky
the evening star has started shining,
instigator of high-flown meditations.

Да, хорошо ты, время. Хорошо
Вдохнуть от твоего ужасного простора.
К чему таиться? Сердце человечье
Играет, как проснувшийся младенец,
Когда война, иль мор, или мятеж
Вдруг налетят и землю сотрясают;
Тут разверзаются, как небо, времена —
И человек душой неутолимой
Бросается в желанную пучину.

Как птица в воздухе, как рыба в океане,
Как скользкий червь в сырых пластах земли,
Как саламандра в пламени – так человек
Во времени. Кочевник полудикий,
По смене лун, по очеркам созвездий
Уже он силится измерить эту бездну
И в письменах неопытных заносит
События, как острова на карте. . .
Но сын отца сменяет. Грады, царства,
Законы, истины – преходят. Человеку
Ломать и строить – равная услада:
Он изобрел историю – он счастлив!
И с ужасом, и с тайным сладострастьем
Следит безумец, как между минувшим
И будущим, подобно ясной влаге,
Сквозь пальцы уходящей, – непрерывно
Жизнь утекает. И трепещет сердце,
Как легкий флаг на мачте корабельной,
Между воспоминаньем и надеждой –
Сей памятью о будущем. . .
                      Но вот –
Шуршат шаги. Горбатая старуха
С большим кулем. Морщинистой рукой
Она со стен сдирает паклю, дранки
Выдергивает. Молча подхожу
И помогаю ей, и мы в согласье добром
Работаем для времени. Темнеет,
Из-за стены встает зеленый месяц
И слабый свет его, как струйка, льется
По кафелям обрушившейся печи.

*2 июля 1919, 12 июня 1920*

*

Yes, Time: you are so good. It's good
to inhale your awful spaciousness.
Why hide the fact? The human heart
is playing like an infant fresh from sleep,
when war, plague, famine, or civil turmoil
swoop down suddenly, and shake the earth;
making the times gape like opening skies
and man, with his soul ever-unsatisfied,
throws himself longingly into the deep.

Like a bird up in the air, a fish in the ocean,
a slippery worm in a damp layer of earth,
like a salamander in flames – man lives
in time. A half-wild nomad, using the moon's
changes and sketched-out constellations,
he makes attempts to measure the abyss,
with his unpractised letters noting down
events like islands plotted on a map. . .
But son displaces father. Cities, empires,
scriptures, truths – they pass away. And man
breaks and builds up again with equal joy.
He's pleased – now he's invented history!
And with both horror and a secret lust
the madman watches how, somewhere between
the past and the future – like clear water
slipping between the fingers – unceasingly
life is trickling away. And the heart flutters
like the flag aloft on the mast of a ship,
between the recollection and the hope
– that memory of a future. . .
                                        But here –
the rustle of footsteps. A hunched old woman
carrying a big sack. With a wrinkled hand
she's ripping down old oakum off the walls,
pulling out laths. I go up silently
to help her, and in pleasant harmony
we do some of the work for time. It's darker:
out from behind the walls a green moon rises,
its feeble light, like a little stream, flows
over the glazed tiles of the tumbled stove.

*2 July 1919, 12 June 1920*

## БЕЗ СЛОВ

Ты показала мне без слов,
Как вышел хорошо и чисто
Тобою проведенный шов
По краю белого батиста.

А я подумал: жизнь моя,
Как нить, за Божьими перстами
По легкой ткани бытия
Бежит такими же стежками.

То виден, то сокрыт стежок,
То в жизнь, то в смерть перебегая. . .
И, улыбаясь, твой платок
Перевернул я, дорогая.

*5–7 апреля 1918*

# Without a Word

Without a word you showed me how
the seam came out so fine and neat,
drawn by your hand along the hem
of cotton cambric, purest white.

And so I thought: that's like my life,
the thread behind God's fingers, which
runs through the insubstantial weave
of being, with a similar stitch.

The stitch now visible, now hidden,
runs through life, and runs through death;
I smiled, and turned your handkerchief,
my dear, to see the underneath.

*5–7 April 1918*

## ГОЛУБОК

Дверцу клетки ты раскрыла.
    Белый голубок
Улетел, в лицо мне бросив
    Быстрый ветерок. . .

Полно! Разве только этот
    Скудный дан мне срок?
Разве, друг мой, ты не вспомнишь
    Эти восемь строк?

*16–17 апреля 1918*


\* \* \*


Я знаю: рук не покладает
В работе мастер гробовой,
А небо все-таки сияет
Над вечною моей Москвой.

И там, где смерть клюкою черной
Стучится в нищие дворы,
Сегодня шумно и задорно
Салазки катятся с горы.

Бегут с корзиной ребятишки,
Вот стали. Бурый снег скрипит: –
И белый голубь из-под крышки
В лазурь морозную летит.

Вот – закружился над Плющихой –
Над снежным полотном реки,
А вслед ему как звонко, лихо
Несутся клики и свистки.

Мальчишки шапками махают,
Алеют лица, как морковь.
Так божества не замечают
За них пролившуюся кровь.

*3 декабря 1917 – январь–февраль 1918*

# The Dove

You opened up the little hatch
    and out the white dove flew,
and as it passed it brushed my face
    as if a stiff breeze blew.

And is that all? This meagre gift
    of time for what I do?
Will you my friend remember these
    eight lines I wrote for you?

*16–17 April 1918*


\* \* \*


I know the coffin-craftsman's working
like a Trojan for the dead,
and yet on my eternal Moscow
heaven is shining overhead.

While death is knocking with his stick
where poorest people dwell together,
now the sledges rumble headlong
down the hillsides, hell for leather.

Children running set a basket
creaking down in browning snow,
and from the lid a dove lifts up
its whiteness to the frosty blue.

It circles round Plyushchíkha, where
a snowy sheet, the river lies;
they trace its progress with resounding
wicked whistling, calls and cries.

Little boys are waving hats,
their cheeks are glowing carrot-red;
like deities, not noticing
it is for them this blood was shed.

*3 December 1917 – January–February 1918*

## МУЗЫКА

Всю ночь мела метель, но утро ясно.
Еще воскресная по телу бродит лень,
У Благовещенья на Бережках обедня
Еще не отошла. Я выхожу во двор.
Как мало всё: и домик, и дымок,
Завившийся над крышей! Сребро-розов
Морозный пар. Столпы его восходят
Из-за домов под самый купол неба,
Как будто крылья ангелов гигантских.
И маленьким таким вдруг оказался
Дородный мой сосед, Сергей Иваныч.
Он в полушубке, в валенках. Дрова
Вокруг него раскиданы по снегу.
Обеими руками, напрягаясь,
Тяжелый свой колун над головою
Заносит он, но – тук! тук! тук! – не громко
Звучат удары: небо, снег и холод
Звук поглощают. . . «С праздником, сосед».
– «А, здравствуйте!» Я тоже расставляю
Свои дрова. Он – тук! Я – тук! Но вскоре
Надоедает мне колоть, я выпрямляюсь
И говорю: «Постойте-ка минутку,
Как будто музыка?» Сергей Иваныч
Перестает работать, голову слегка
Приподымает, ничего не слышит,
Но слушает старательно. . . «Должно быть,
Вам показалось», – говорит он. «Что вы,
Да вы прислушайтесь. Так ясно слышно!»
Он слушает опять: «Ну, может быть –
Военного хоронят? Только что-то
Мне не слыхать». Но я не унимаюсь:
«Помилуйте, теперь совсем уж ясно.
И музыка идет как будто сверху.
Виолончель. . . и арфы, может быть. . .
Вот хорошо играют! Не стучите».
И бедный мой Сергей Иваныч снова
Перестает колоть. Он ничего не слышит,
Но мне мешать не хочет и досады

# The Music

Blizzards whirled all night, but morning's clear.
A Sunday laziness creeps through my body;
the Church of the Annunciation not yet
out of mass. I go out to the yard.
How small, all of it: a little house, a little
twist of smoke above the roof! Silvery-rosy
frost vapour. Pillars of it rise from
behind the houses, up to the dome of heaven
as if they were the wings of giant angels.
And suddenly how miniature he's turned,
the man next door, burly Sergey Ivanych.
There he is, in sheepskin coat and felt boots.
Firewood scattered round him in the snow.
With both his arms tensing as he raises
the heavy chopper up above his head, he
swings it – but *Tock! Tock! Tock!* goes each
unresounding blow: sky, snow and cold
are swallowing the sound. . . 'Greetings, neighbour.'
'Ah, good morning!' – and I sort out my own
firewood, too. His *Tock!* My *Tock!* But it soon
gets on my nerves, chopping. I straighten up,
saying 'Hang on there a minute, isn't that
some kind of music?' Sergey Ivanych
pauses in his work, lifts up his head
just a little – nothing he can hear, but
he's trying hard to listen for it. . . 'Must have
imagined it,' he tells me. 'No, but look,
get yourself attuned. You'll hear it clearly!'
He's listening again. 'Well, maybe – are they
burying a soldier? Only somehow I
can't make it out.' But I don't let it go.
'Forgive me, but now it's really clear.
And it's as if the music's overhead.
I hear a cello. . . there are harps, perhaps. . .
Really fine musicianship! Stop bashing –'
Sergey Ivanych, poor man, once again
holds off from chopping. He can't hear a thing,

Старается не выказать. Забавно:
Стоит он посреди двора, боясь нарушить
Неслышную симфонию. И жалко
Мне наконец становится его.
Я объявляю: «Кончилось!» Мы снова
За топоры беремся. Тук! Тук! Тук!.. А небо
Такое же высокое, и так же
В нем ангелы пернатые сияют.

*15 июня 1920*


\* \* \*


Леди долго руки мыла,
Леди крепко руки терла.
Эта леди не забыла
Окровавленного горла.

Леди, леди! Вы как птица
Бьетесь на бессонном ложе.
Триста лет уж вам не спится –
Мне лет шесть не спится тоже.

*9 января 1922*

but wishing not to spoil it for me, tries hard
not to look annoyed. Funny: he's standing
there in the middle of the yard, afraid to disturb
an inaudible symphony. And I regret,
eventually, the way I've made him stop.
I declare: 'It's finished.' Once again we
get down to our axes: *Tock! Tock! Tock!* – while
the sky stays as high as ever, and up there
still the same, the feathery angels shining.

*15 June 1920*

\* \* \*

Lady's washed her hands so long,
lady's scrubbed her hands so hard,
and this lady won't forget
the blood around the neck.

Lady, lady! Like a bird
you twitch about your sleepless bed.
Three hundred years you've had no sleep –
and six years now I've stayed awake.

*9 January 1922*

* * *

Не матерью, но тульскою крестьянкой
Еленой Кузиной я выкормлен. Она
Свивальники мне грела над лежанкой,
Крестила на ночь от дурного сна.

Она не знала сказок и не пела,
Зато всегда хранила для меня
В заветном сундуке, обитом жестью белой,
То пряник вяземский, то мятного коня.

Она меня молитвам не учила,
Но отдала мне безраздельно всё:
И материнство горькое свое,
И просто всё, что дорого ей было.

Лишь раз, когда упал я из окна,
Но встал живой (как помню этот день я!),
Грошовую свечу за чудное спасенье
У Иверской поставила она.

И вот, Россия, «громкая держава»,
Ее сосцы губами теребя,
Я высосал мучительное право
Тебя любить и проклинать тебя.

В том честном подвиге, в том счастье песнопений,
Которому служу я в каждый миг,
Учитель мой — твой чудотворный гений,
И поприще — волшебный твой язык.

И пред твоими слабыми сынами
Еще порой гордиться я могу,
Что сей язык, завещанный веками,
Любовней и ревнивей берегу. . .

* * *

Not my mother, but a Tula peasant,
Yeléna Kúzina, fed me her breast.
She warmed my swaddling-clothes above the stove,
and with her cross at night my dreams were blessed.

She knew no fairy tales and never sang:
but always kept as treats for me instead
inside her treasured white enamel tin
a peppermint horse or fruity gingerbread.

She never taught me how to say my prayers,
but gave up everything she had for me:
including her own bitter motherhood,
all that was dear to her, unconditionally.

Only the time I tumbled from the window, but
stood up alive (that day for ever mine!),
she offered her two kopeks for a candle
lit for the miracle, at Mary's shrine.

And as for you, great Russia, 'thundering power':
taking her nipples for my lips to pull,
I suckled the excruciating right
to love you, and to curse at you as well.

My honest, joyful task of making psalms,
in which I serve each moment all day long,
your wonder-making genius teaches me,
and my profession is your magic tongue.

And I may stand before your feeble sons
priding myself at times that I can guard
this language, handed down from age to age,
with a more jealous love for every word. . .

Года бегут. Грядущего не надо,
Минувшее в душе пережжено,
Но тайная жива еще отрада,
Что есть и мне прибежище одно:

Там, где на сердце, съеденном червями,
Любовь ко мне нетленно затая,
Спит рядом с царскими, ходынскими гостями
Елена Кузина, кормилица моя.

*12 февраля 1917, 2 марта 1922*

The years fly by. The future has no use,
the past has burnt itself into my soul.
And yet the secret joy is still alive,
for me there is one refuge from it all:

where lies the still imperishable love
even a maggot-eaten heart can keep:
beside the trampled coronation crowd
my nurse, Yelena Kuzina, asleep.

*12 February 1917, 2 March 1922*

\* \* \*

Люблю людей, люблю природу,
Но не люблю ходить гулять,
И твердо знаю, что народу
Моих творений не понять.

Довольный малым, созерцаю
То, что дает нещедрый рок:
Вяз, прислонившийся к сараю,
Покрытый лесом бугорок...

Ни грубой славы, ни гонений
От современников не жду,
Но сам стригу кусты сирени
Вокруг террасы и в саду.

*15–16 июня 1921*

* * *

I love the world, its people, nature,
but don't care to promenade,
and folk, I know, will fail to see
the point of what my art has made.

Happy with little, I observe
the gifts of fate's ungenerous hand:
the elm that leans against the shed,
the forest on the rising land.

From my contemporaries I don't
expect crude fame, nor persecution;
I shall quietly trim the lilacs
round the terrace and the garden.

*15–16 June 1921*

## ГОСТЮ

Входя ко мне, неси мечту,
Иль дьявольскую красоту,
Иль Бога, если сам ты Божий.
А маленькую доброту,
Как шляпу, оставляй в прихожей.

Здесь, на горошине земли,
Будь или ангел, или демон.
А человек – иль не затем он,
Чтобы забыть его могли?

*7 июля 1921*

## ЖИЗЕЛЬ

Да, да! В слепой и нежной страсти
Переболей, перегори,
Рви сердце, как письмо, на части,
Сойди с ума, потом умри.

И что ж? Могильный камень двигать
Опять придется над собой,
Опять любить и ножкой дрыгать
На сцене лунно-голубой.

*1 мая 1922*

# To the Visitor

Enter bringing me a dream,
or some gorgeousness from Hell,
or bring me God if you're from Him,
but little acts of meaning well
leave on the hatstand in the hall.

Here on this pea we call the Earth,
either be angel or be demon,
but to be human – what's the worth
of that, except to be forgotten?

*7 July 1921*

# Giselle

Yes, yes! In blind and tender passion
wear out the pain, burn out the fire;
rip your heart up, like a letter,
lose your mind, and then expire.

And then? Once more to roll away
the gravestone that lies over you;
to love once more, and flash your feet
upon a stage of moonlit blue.

*1 May 1922*

# ИЗ ОКНА

## 1

Нынче день такой забавный:
От возниц, что было сил,
Конь умчался своенравный;
Мальчик змей свой упустил;
Вор цыпленка утащил
У безносой Николавны.

Но – настигнут вор нахальный,
Змей упал в соседний сад,
Мальчик ладит хвост мочальный,
И коня ведут назад:
Восстает мой тихий ад
В стройности первоначальной.

*23 июля 1921*

## 2

Всё жду: кого-нибудь задавит
Взбесившийся автомобиль,
Зевака бледный окровавит
Торцовую сухую пыль.

И с этого пойдет, начнется:
Раскачка, выворот, беда,
Звезда на землю оборвется,
И станет горькою вода.

Прервутся сны, что душу душат.
Начнется всё, чего хочу,
И солнце ангелы потушат,
Как утром – лишнюю свечу.

*11 августа 1921*
*Бельское Устье*

# From the Window

### 1

Today was such a funny day:
the carter's carthorse ran away
to please himself, and let it rip;
a kite escaped a young boy's grip;
no-nose Nikolavna grieved
because her chicken had been thieved.

But now the thief is going to jail;
the kite fell in the yard next door
– the boy is primping up its tail;
the horse is back at home once more:
the quiet harmony of my hell
has been restored, and all is well.

*23 July 1921*

### 2

Always I expect the worst:
a speeding car gone raving mad
will leave you gaping in the dust
that soaks away your gushing blood.

And this is how it's going to start:
diversions, dizziness, distress,
a broken star falls down to earth,
the waters turn to bitterness.

Soul-choking dreams are over and done,
and all I wish for is beginning:
angels will put out the sun
like a candle in the morning.

*11 August 1921*
*Bel'skoye Ust'ye*

# СТАНСЫ

Бывало, думал: ради мига
И год, и два, и жизнь отдам. . .
Цены не знает прощелыга
Своим приблудным пятакам.

Теперь иные дни настали.
Лежат морщины возле губ,
Мои минуты вздорожали,
Я стал умен, суров и скуп.

Я много вижу, много знаю,
Моя седеет голова,
И звездный ход я примечаю,
И слышу, как растет трава.

И каждый вам неслышный шепот,
И каждый вам незримый свет
Обогащают смутный опыт
Психеи, падающей в бред.

Теперь себя я не обижу:
Старею, горблюсь, – но коплю
Всё, что так нежно ненавижу
И так язвительно люблю.

*17–18 августа 1922*
*Misdroy*

# Stanzas

I thought once: for a moment's sake,
a year, a life I'd sacrifice. . .
How can a spendthrift know the worth
of any stray five-kopek piece?

But lines have settled round my mouth
and other days have come to be.
Each minute's value has increased:
I'm wise, severe, and miserly.

My hair is grey, I've seen so much,
by now there is so much I know,
I track the movement of the stars,
I hear the way the grasses grow.

And every whisper you can't hear
and every glimmer you can't see
enriches the delirious whirl
of Psyche's dark insanity.

And now I don't begrudge myself:
older and stooped, I start to hoard
all that I've tenderly despised
and so sarcastically adored.

*17–18 August 1922*
*Misdroy*

## ПРОБОЧКА

Пробочка над крепким йодом!
Как ты скоро перетлела!
Так вот и душа незримо
Жжет и разъедает тело.

*17 сентября 1921*
*Бельское Устье*


## ИЗ ДНЕВНИКА

Мне каждый звук терзает слух,
И каждый луч глазам несносен.
Прорезываться начал дух,
Как зуб из-под припухших десен.

Прорежется – и сбросит прочь
Изношенную оболочку.
Тысячеокий – канет в ночь,
Не в эту серенькую ночку.

А я останусь тут лежать –
Банкир, заколотый апашем, –
Руками рану зажимать,
Кричать и биться в мире вашем.

*18 июня 1921*

# The Stopper

The stopper on the iodine
has rotted from the strength inside;
that's how the soul will burn unseen
and eat the flesh it's occupied.

*17 September 1921*
*Bel'skoye Ust'ye*

# From the Diary

Every sound torments my ears;
every sunbeam hurts my eyes.
Like a tooth through swollen gums
the spirit has begun to rise.

It's cutting through – and now it throws
this worn-out envelope away.
Night shall devour its many eyes,
and not this twilight, dull and grey.

I'm like a banker, left to die
the victim of a gangster's knife,
with only hands to stanch the wound –
in this, your world, I fight for life.

*18 June 1921*

## ЛАСТОЧКИ

Имей глаза – сквозь день увидишь ночь,
Не озаренную тем воспаленным диском.
Две ласточки напрасно рвутся прочь,
Перед окном шныряя с тонким писком.

Вон ту прозрачную, но прочную плеву
Не прободать крылом остроугольным,
Не выпорхнуть туда, за синеву,
Ни птичьим крылышком, ни сердцем подневольным.

Пока вся кровь не выступит из пор,
Пока не выплачешь земные очи –
Не станешь духом. Жди, смотря в упор,
Как брызжет свет, не застилая ночи.

*18–24 июня 1921*

# The Swallows

If you have eyes – through day you'll see a night
the rays from that inflaming disc won't reach.
A pair of swallows fighting to escape
flap at the window, where they feebly cheep.

But that transparent yet unyielding sheet
was never cut by wings, however sharp;
no darting that way out into the blue,
with any tiny wing, or captive heart.

Until the blood issues from every pore,
until you've wept away your earthly sight,
you can't become a spirit. Wait, and stare
at how a splash of light won't hide the night.

*18–24 June 1921*

* * *

Перешагни, перескочи,
Перелети, пере- что хочешь –
Но вырвись: камнем из пращи,
Звездой, сорвавшейся в ночи. . .
Сам затерял – теперь ищи. . .

Бог знает, что́ себе бормочешь,
Ища пенсне или ключи.

*Весна 1921, 11 января 1922*


## СУМЕРКИ

Снег навалил. Всё затихает, глохнет.
Пустынный тянется вдоль переулка дом.
Вот человек идет. Пырнуть его ножом –
К забору прислонится и не охнет.
Потом опустится и ляжет вниз лицом.
И ветерка дыханье снеговое,
И вечера чуть уловимый дым –
Предвестники прекрасного покоя –
Свободно так закружатся над ним.
А люди черными сбегутся муравьями
Из улиц, со дворов, и станут между нами.
И будут спрашивать, за что и как убил, –
И не поймет никто, как я его любил.

*5 ноября 1921*

\* \* \*

Step over, leap across,
fly beyond, however you like, get through it –
but tear yourself off: be a stone from a sling,
be a star that breaks away from the night. . .
You lost it yourself – now look for it.

God knows what you grunt to yourself,
looking for spectacles or keys.

*Spring 1921; 11 January 1922*

# Twilight

Snow piled up. Everything deadening down.
A stretch of lane beside an empty house.
A man is walking there. If someone knifed him
he'd slump against the fence without a groan.
Then he'd sink and lie upon his face.
And there's the snowy breathing of the breeze
and smoke of evening only just begun,
heralding a lovely time of rest –
how freely they begin to whirl above him.
People in black like ants come running out
from streets, from courtyards, and will stand between us.
And they're asking why and how I killed him –
and no one understands how much I loved him.

*5 November 1921*

## БЕЛЬСКОЕ УСТЬЕ

Здесь даль видна в просторной раме:
За речкой луг, за лугом лес.
Здесь ливни черными столпами
Проходят по краям небес.

Здесь радуга высоким сводом
Церковный покрывает крест
И каждый праздник по приходам
Справляют ярмарки невест.

Здесь аисты, болота, змеи,
Крутой песчаный косогор,
Простые сельские затеи,
Об урожае разговор.

А я росистые поляны
Топчу тяжелым башмаком,
Я петербургские туманы
Таю любовно под плащом,

И к девушкам, румяным розам,
Склоняясь томною главой,
Дышу на них туберкулезом,
И вдохновеньем, и Невой,

И мыслю: что ж, таков от века,
От самых роковых времен,
Для ангела и человека
Непререкаемый закон.

И тот, прекрасный неудачник
С печатью знанья на челе,
Был тоже – просто первый дачник
На расцветающей земле.

Сойдя с возвышенного Града
В долину мирных райских роз,
И он дыхание распада
На крыльях дымчатых принес.

*31 декабря 1921*
*Петербург*

# Bel'skoye Ust'ye

Here's the spacious prospect framed:
river, then meadow, then woods beyond meadow.
Downpours pass on heaven's edge,
rows of columns dark in shadow.

Here the vaulting rainbow takes
the church's cross within its range,
and every parish holiday
brings business for the bride exchange.

Here are the storks, the marsh, the snakes,
the steepness of the sandy bluff,
the simple countryside concerns
with talk of crops and farming stuff.

And here I am in dewy glades,
to trample with my heavy boot,
and bring the fogs of Petersburg
lovingly hidden in my coat,

and to the blushing rosy maidens
languidly nodding, I exhale
tuberculosis, inspiration,
Nevá miasmas, cold and pale.

I think: that's how it's always been
from the most fateful time of all
for angels and for humankind,
the most unquestionable law.

Like me, that gorgeous fallen one
with knowledge stamped across his face
was simply the first vacationer
on earth, that freshly-blooming place.

From the celestial city, down
to rosy paradise on earth,
descending on his smoky wings
he brought decay upon his breath.

*31 December 1921*
*Petersburg*

\* \* \*

Играю в карты, пью вино,
С людьми живу – и лба не хмурю.
Ведь знаю: сердце всё равно
Летит в излюбленную бурю.

Лети, кораблик мой, лети,
Кренясь и не ища спасенья.
Его и нет на том пути,
Куда уносит вдохновенье.

Уж не вернуться нам назад,
Хотя в ненастье нашей ночи,
Быть может, с берега глядят
Одни нам ведомые очи.

А нет – беды не много в том!
Забыты мы – и то не плохо.
Ведь мы и гибнем и поём
Не для девического вздоха.

*4–6 февраля 1922*
*Москва*

* * *

I play at cards, I drink my wine,
I live with people, do not frown,
because I know my steady heart
will fly along, it loves the storm.

Speed on, my little ship, speed on
though listing, and not seeking rescue.
There's no safety to be found
the way your inspiration takes you.

And there's no turning back for us
although, throughout our stormy night,
perhaps there are some eyes we know
on shore, that keep us in their sight.

If not, that's no calamity!
It's not so bad they've passed us by.
We're singing as we're sinking, but
it isn't for a maiden's sigh.

*4–6 February 1922*
*Moscow*

# АВТОМОБИЛЬ

Бредем в молчании суровом.
Сырая ночь, пустая мгла.
И вдруг – с каким певучим зовом –
Автомобиль из-за угла.

Он черным лаком отливает,
Сияя гранями стекла,
Он в сумрак ночи простирает
Два белых ангельских крыла.

И стали здания похожи
На праздничные стены зал,
И близко возле нас прохожий
Сквозь эти крылья пробежал.

А свет мелькнул и замаячил,
Колебля дождевую пыль. . .
Но слушай: мне являться начал
Другой, другой автомобиль. . .

Он пробегает в ясном свете,
Он пробегает белым днем,
И два крыла на нем, как эти,
Но крылья черные на нем.

И всё, что только попадает
Под черный сноп его лучей,
Невозвратимо исчезает
Из утлой памяти моей.

Я забываю, я теряю
Психею светлую мою,
Слепые руки простираю,
И ничего не узнаю:

Здесь мир стоял, простой и целый,
Но с той поры, как ездит *тот*,
В душе и в мире есть пробелы,
Как бы от пролитых кислот.

*2–5 декабря 1921*

# The Automobile

We're shuffling on in solemn silence.
Damp and gloom. Night without end.
But suddenly – so melodiously –
an automobile comes round the bend.

Its paint of shimmering glossy black,
its crystal facets shining bright;
into the dark it stretches out
two broad angelic wings of white.

And now the buildings in the street
seem decked with festive garlandings,
and someone passing hurriedly
has run clean through the ghostly wings.

The light has flashed and disappeared,
scattering drops of rainy spray.
But listen, I feel another, different
automobile now comes this way.

It rushes through the brightest sunshine,
through the light of day it goes
upon another pair of wings,
but these are blacker than a crow's.

And everything that falls beneath
the beam of dark its headlamps shed
irrevocably disappears
from out of my enfeebled head.

I have forgotten, I have lost
bright Psyche with her shining eyes;
I stretch out blind and helpless hands,
there's nothing I can recognize.

A simple world stood here, intact,
but once this car arrived, our souls
and all our world have been as if
splattered with acid, full of holes.

*2–5 December 1921*

* * *

На тускнеющие шпили,
На верхи автомобилей,
На железо старых стрех
Налипает первый снег.

Много раз я это видел,
А потом возненавидел,
Но сегодня тот же вид
Новым чем-то веселит.

Это сам я в год минувший,
В Божьи бездны соскользнувший,
Пересоздал навсегда
Мир, державшийся года.

И вот в этом мире новом,
Напряженном и суровом,
Нынче выпал первый снег...
Не такой он, как у всех.

*24 октября 1921*

* * *

Onto the tarnished spires,
onto the tops of cars,
onto the old iron eaves
the early snow adheres.

Many times I've seen this
until it's come to bore me,
but that hated sight today
has something new to cheer me.

This past year, my usual self
slipped into God's own pit,
but took the never-changing world
and recreated it.

And now into this new-made world,
difficult and austere,
for me, though not for everyone,
a different snow is here.

*24 October 1921*

* * *

Гляжу на грубые ремесла,
Но знаю твердо: мы в раю. . .
Простой рыбак бросает весла
И ржавый якорь на скамью.

Потом с товарищем толкает
Ладью тяжелую с песков
И против солнца уплывает
Далеко на вечерний лов.

И там, куда смотреть нам больно,
Где плещут волны в небосклон,
Высокий парус трехугольный
Легко развертывает он.

Тогда встает в дали далекой
Розовоперое крыло.
Ты скажешь: ангел там высокий
Ступил на воды тяжело.

И непоспешными стопами
Другие подошли к нему,
Шатая плавными крылами
Морскую дымчатую тьму.

Клубятся облака густые,
Дозором ангелы встают, –
И кто поверит, что простые
Там сети и ладьи плывут?

*19–20 августа 1922*
*Misdroy*

* * *

I watch the humble working men,
and know that heaven is here, and ours. . .
The simple fisherman throws on deck
the rusty anchor and the oars.

Then with his mates he shoves the boat
to shift its weight from off the sands,
and sails away towards the sun
to see what fish the evening lands.

It hurts our eyes to turn towards
the line of waves that meet the sky
where easily he now unfurls
his sail, triangular and high.

And then a rosy-feathered wing
far in the distance rises up.
You'll say: a lofty angel walks
the water with a heavy step.

And others making their approach
to join the first, unhurriedly,
are ruffling with their flowing wings
the smoky darkness of the sea.

The thickening clouds are in a swirl;
angels are rising on patrol,
and who would think, among them, simple
boats with nets are setting sail?

*19–20 August 1922*
*Misdroy*

## БАЛЛАДА

Сижу, освещаемый сверху,
Я в комнате круглой моей.
Смотрю в штукатурное небо
На солнце в шестнадцать свечей.

Кругом – освещенные тоже,
И стулья, и стол, и кровать.
Сижу – и в смущенье не знаю,
Куда бы мне руки девать.

Морозные белые пальмы
На стеклах беззвучно цветут.
Часы с металлическим шумом
В жилетном кармане идут.

О, косная, нищая скудость
Безвыходной жизни моей!
Кому мне поведать, как жалко
Себя и всех этих вещей?

И я начинаю качаться,
Колени обнявши свои,
И вдруг начинаю стихами
С собой говорить в забытьи.

Бессвязные, страстные речи!
Нельзя в них понять ничего,
Но звуки правдивее смысла,
И слово сильнее всего.

И музыка, музыка, музыка
Вплетается в пенье мое,
И узкое, узкое, узкое
Пронзает меня лезвиё.

# Ballad of the Heavy Lyre

I sit where the light is above me,
my circular room is my sphere;
I gaze at a plasterwork heaven
where the sun is an old chandelier.

And likewise illumined around me,
the chairs and the table and bed.
Should I sit with my hands in my pockets,
or where might I put them instead?

Silently, frost on the window
grows palm-trees and icy white flowers;
my watch ticks away in my waistcoat,
metallically counting the hours.

Oh my life is so worthless, a quagmire
where I'm stuck with no way to get free!
And who can I tell of my pity
for the things that I own, and for me?

And hugging my knees where I'm sitting,
I'm rocking, quite gently at first,
when out of the trance that I've entered
a chorus of verses has burst.

It's nothing but passionate nonsense!
Whatever it means, it's absurd,
but sound is more honest than meaning,
and strongest of all is a word.

And a music, the music of music
is twined in the song of my life,
and piercing me, piercing and piercing,
is the blade of the slenderest knife.

Я сам над собой вырастаю,
Над мертвым встаю бытием,
Стопами в подземное пламя,
В текучие звезды челом.

И вижу большими глазами –
Глазами, быть может, змеи, –
Как пению дикому внемлют
Несчастные вещи мои.

И в плавный, вращательный танец
Вся комната мерно идет,
И кто-то тяжелую лиру
Мне в руки сквозь ветер дает.

И нет штукатурного неба
И солнца в шестнадцать свечей:
На гладкие черные скалы
Стопы опирает – Орфей.

*9–22 декабря 1921*

I find myself rising above me,
from where I exist but am dead;
my feet are in underground fire,
and a galaxy streams at my head.

I watch with my eyes ever wider –
how a serpent might see through the gloom –
I see my wild song is entrancing
the comfortless things in my room,

and the things begin dancing a measure,
with gracefully circling charms;
and somebody's heavy lyre comes
from out of the wind to my arms.

And there is no plasterwork heaven,
no chandelier sun any more;
but the blackness of slippery boulders
and Orpheus, his feet on the shore.

*9–22 December 1921*

# ПЕТЕРБУРГ

Напастям жалким и однообразным
Там предавались до потери сил.
Один лишь я полуживым соблазном
Средь озабоченных ходил.

Смотрели на меня – и забывали
Клокочущие чайники свои;
На печках валенки сгорали;
Все слушали стихи мои.

А мне тогда в тьме гробовой, российской,
Являлась вестница в цветах,
И лад открылся музикийский
Мне в сногсшибательных ветрах.

И я безумел от видений,
Когда чрез ледяной канал,
Скользя с обломанных ступеней,
Треску зловонную таскал,

И, каждый стих гоня сквозь прозу,
Вывихивая каждую строку,
Привил-таки классическую розу
К советскому дичку.

*12 декабря 1925*
*Chaville*

# Petersburg

They gave themselves to sad monotonous
tasks, until their strength was spent.
Half-dead among them, only I
distracted their predicament.

They looked at me and they forgot
their bubbling kettles boiling dry,
the boots of felt that scorched on stoves
– all listening to my poetry.

Then in sepulchral Russian dark
a flowery herald-girl took my hand;
and music's concord was revealed
to me, knocked sideways in the wind.

Mad with visions, over the sheet-ice
on the canal, I'd reach the bank
and slither up the crumbling steps
clutching a piece of cod that stank,

and driving every verse through prose
disjointed in the pull and push,
somehow I grafted the classic rose
to the Soviet briar bush.

*12 December 1925*
*Chaville*

* * *

Жив Бог! Умен, а не заумен,
Хожу среди своих стихов,
Как непоблажливый игумен
Среди смиренных чернецов.
Пасу послушливое стадо
Я процветающим жезлом.
Ключи таинственного сада
Звенят на поясе моем.
Я – чающий и говорящий.
Заумно, может быть, поет
Лишь ангел, Богу предстоящий, –
Да Бога не узревший скот
Мычит заумно и ревет.
А я – не ангел осиянный,
Не лютый змий, не глупый бык.
Люблю из рода в род мне данный
Мой человеческий язык:
Его суровую свободу,
Его извилистый закон. . .
О, если б мой предсмертный стон
Облечь в отчетливую оду!

*4 февраля – 13 мая 1923*
*Saarow*

\* \* \*

God alive! I'm not beyond coherence:
mindfully, I walk among my poems
like a disobliging abbot
among his humble monks.
I shepherd my obedient flock
with a staff that's bursting into bloom.
The keys to the mysterious garden
hang clinking at my belt.
I ponder hopefully, I pronounce.
Metalogical? Maybe the angel
that stands in the presence of God to sing,
or the oxen that don't even recognize God,
way beyond thought as they moo and bellow.
But I'm no angel of brightness,
no cruel serpent, no idiot bull.
From generation to generation
this human language has been spoken:
I love its rigorous freedom,
I love its twisting laws. . .
O may my last expiring groan
be wrapped inside an articulate ode!

*4 February – 13 March 1923*
*Saarow*

* * *

Весенний лепет не разнежит
Сурово стиснутых стихов.
Я полюбил железный скрежет
Какофонических миров.

В зиянии разверстых гласных
Дышу легко и вольно я.
Мне чудится в толпе согласных –
Льдин взгроможденных толчея.

Мне мил – из оловянной тучи
Удар изломанной стрелы,
Люблю певучий и визгучий
Лязг электрической пилы.

И в этой жизни мне дороже
Всех гармонических красот –
Дрожь, побежавшая по коже,
Иль ужаса холодный пот,

Иль сон, где, некогда единый, –
Взрываясь, разлетаюсь я,
Как грязь, разбрызганная шиной
По чуждым сферам бытия.

*24–27 марта 1923*
*Saarow*

* * *

The babble of spring won't melt the glue
of strictly dovetailed prosody.
I've come to love the iron grind
when worlds are in cacophony.

The vowels that gape with open mouths
can let me breathe, and freely speak;
in crowds of consonants I hear
the pack-ice chunks that crunch and creak.

I love a tin-drum cloud that shoots
its jagged arrows to the ground;
and sweet to me the electric saw,
its singing, screaming, scraping sound.

For all the lovely harmonies
here in this life, I value dearer
shudders that ripple through my flesh,
the sweaty clamminess of horror,

or dreams in which from being whole,
I burst and splatter everywhere
like mud that's flinging from a tyre,
whirled off toward some alien sphere.

*24–27 March 1923*
*Saarow*

## БЕРЛИНСКОЕ

Что ж? От озноба и простуды –
Горячий грог или коньяк.
Здесь музыка, и звон посуды,
И лиловатый полумрак.

А там, за толстым и огромным
Отполированным стеклом,
Как бы в аквариуме темном,
В аквариуме голубом –

Многоочитые трамваи
Плывут между подводных лип,
Как электрические стаи
Светящихся ленивых рыб.

И там, скользя в ночную гнилость,
На толще чуждого стекла
В вагонных окнах отразилась
Поверхность моего стола, –

И проникая в жизнь чужую,
Вдруг с отвращеньем узнаю
Отрубленную, неживую,
Ночную голову мою.

*14–24 сентября 1922*
*Берлин*

# Berlin View

So? For the shivering and the sneezing,
hot toddy, cognac, rum;
music, and chinking cups and saucers,
here in the violet semi-gloom.

Behind the thick expanse of polished
plate-glass window, there's a view
as if of a dark aquarium,
a dim aquarium of blue:

and through the underwater lindens
floating tramcars, many-eyed,
like luminous electric shoals
of fish that nonchalantly glide.

And sliding through the stagnant night
the tramcar windows as they pass
reflect my café tabletop
in every alien pane of glass.

And while I'm gazing at this alien
life, I jolt, to find instead
I'm sickened by the severed, lifeless
night-stricken image of my head.

*14–24 September 1922*
*Berlin*

## ДАЧНОЕ

Уродики, уродища, уроды
Весь день озерные мутили воды.

Теперь над озером ненастье, мрак,
В траве – лягушечий зеленый квак.

Огни на дачах гаснут понемногу,
Клубки червей полезли на дорогу,

А вдалеке, где всё затерла мгла,
Тупая граммофонная игла

Шатается по рытвинам царапин,
И из трубы еще рычит Шаляпин.

На мокрый мир нисходит угомон. . .
Лишь кое-где, топча сырой газон,

Блудливые невесты с женихами
Слипаются, накрытые зонтами,

А к ним под юбки лазит с фонарем
Полуслепой, широкоротый гном.

*10 июня 1923*
*Saarow*

*31 августа 1924*
*Causeway*

# At the Dachas

Monsters, monsters' sons and monsters' daughters
have made a mess all day upon the waters.

But now above the lake there's rain and dark,
and from the grass a green amphibian croak.

The dachas one by one put out their lights,
the worms come out to crawl about in knots,

while in the distance, where the gloom has grown,
the blunted needle of the gramophone

wobbles around the record, scratched and worn,
to keep Chaliapin growling through the horn.

The sodden world finds peace descend at last
except that here and there, flattening the grass

under umbrellas, girls and their young men
lustfully cling to keep out of the rain,

and lurking with a lamp to take a peep
a half-blind grinning gnome begins to creep.

*10 June 1923*
*Saarow*

*31 August 1924*
*[Giant's] Causeway*

\* \* \*

Встаю расслабленный с постели.
Не с Богом бился я в ночи, –
Но тайно сквозь меня летели
Колючих радио лучи.

И мнится: где-то в теле живы,
Бегут по жилам до сих пор
Москвы бунтарские призывы
И бирж всесветный разговор.

Незаглушимо и сумбурно
Пересеклись в моей тиши
Ночные голоса Мельбурна
С ночными знаньями души.

И чьи-то имена и цифры
Вонзаются в разъятый мозг,
Врываются в глухие шифры
Разряды океанских гроз.

Хожу – и в ужасе внимаю
Шум, не внимаемый никем.
Руками уши зажимаю –
Всё тот же звук! А между тем. . .

О, если бы вы знали сами,
Европы темные сыны,
Какими вы *еще* лучами
Неощутимо пронзены!

*5–10 февраля 1923*
*Saarow*

* * *

I get up weakened from my bed.
It wasn't God I fought last night –
but prickly rays of radio
shot through me on their secret flight.

All the time, it seems, they run
inside the body's living dwelling:
Moscow's turbulent rallying-cries
and all the talk the world is selling.

Over my rest they have traversed,
chaotic, undiscernible,
Melbourne's night-time voices crossed
with night-time secrets of my soul.

And random names and numbers bruise
my open brain, exposed to notions,
undecipherable code,
the crashing thunder of the oceans.

Walking in horror, I can hear
a noise that no one knew before.
I press my hands against my ears –
again that sound! But furthermore. . .

O sons of European dark,
if only you already knew
that, imperceptibly to you,
more rays will come to pierce you through!

*5–10 February 1923*
*Saarow*

## СОРРЕНТИНСКИЕ ФОТОГРАФИИ

Воспоминанье прихотливо
И непослушливо. Оно –
Как узловатая олива:
Никак, ничем не стеснено.
Свои причудливые ветви
Узлами диких соответствий
Нерасторжимо заплетет –
И так живет, и так растет.

Порой фотограф-ротозей
Забудет снимкам счет и пленкам
И снимет парочку друзей,
На Капри, с беленьким козленком, –
И тут же, пленки не сменив,
Запечатлеет он залив
За пароходною кормою
И закопченную трубу
С космою дымною на лбу.
Так сделал нынешней зимою
Один приятель мой. Пред ним
Смешались воды, люди, дым
На негативе помутнелом.
Его знакомый легким телом
Полупрозрачно заслонял
Черты скалистых исполинов,
А козлик, ноги в небо вскинув,
Везувий рожками бодал. . .
Хоть я и не люблю козляток
(Ни итальянских пикников) –
Двух совместившихся миров
Мне полюбился отпечаток:
В себе виденья затая,
Так протекает жизнь моя.

\*

Я вижу скалы и агавы,
А в них, сквозь них и между них –

# Sorrento Photographs

Memory takes capricious chances
never wanting to be told
what it must do – the way an old
contorted olive twists its branches,
growing oddly as it weaves
its net of wildly spreading plaits
in never-disentangled knots –
that's how the olive grows, and lives.

Photographers at times forget
how many frames the counter shows:
a scatterbrain takes friends who pose
on Capri with a little goat,
and doesn't give the wheel a turn
before the next shot, on the boat;
snapping the bay beyond the stern
behind the funnel, caked with soot
and coiffured with a smoky fringe
– a trick a friend of mine performed
this very winter. People swarmed
in sea and smoke, a rich and strange
amalgam on his photograph.
His friend's unearthly body, half-
transparent, came to interrupt
the outline of the giant crags
at which the kid threw out its legs
and gave Vesuvius a butt. . .
Though little goats don't interest me
(nor picnicking in Italy),
I liked the print of overlapping
double worlds, the outer wrapping
over visions of their own,
for that's the way my life has run.

*

Among the rocks, agaves grow

Домишко низкий и плюгавый,
Обитель прачек и портных.
И как ни отвожу я взора,
Он всё маячит предо мной,
Как бы сползая с косогора
Над мутною Москвой-рекой.
И на зеленый, величавый
Амальфитанский перевал
Он жалкой тенью набежал,
Стопою нищенскою стал
На пласт окаменелой лавы.

Раскрыта дверь в полуподвал,
И в сокрушении глубоком
Четыре прачки, полубоком,
Выносят из сеней во двор
На полотенцах гроб дощатый,
В гробу – Савельев, полотер.
На нем – потертый, полосатый
Пиджак. Икона на груди
Под бородою рыжеватой.
«Ну, Ольга, полно. Выходи».
И Ольга, прачка, за перила
Хватаясь крепкою рукой,
Выходит. И заголосила.
И тронулись под женский вой
Неспешно со двора долой.
И сквозь колючие агавы
Они выходят из ворот,
И полотера лоб курчавый
В лазурном воздухе плывет.
И, от мечты не отрываясь,
Я сам, в оливковом саду,
За смутным шествием иду,
О чуждый камень спотыкаясь.

\*

Мотоциклетка стрекотнула
И сорвалась. Затрепетал
Прожектор по уступам скал,
И отзвук рокота и гула

and in them, through them, in between
I see a hovel, mean abode
of those who wash and clean and sew;
and though I turn my gaze aside
it comes back miserably again
as if it were about to slide
down to the Moscow River's mud.
On the stately slopes of green
above Amalfi's deep ravine,
its wretched shade loomed up for me
to bring its beggarly foot to land
on lava turned to solid ground.

A door is open down some steps.
Four washerwomen in the depths
of grieving carry, awkwardly
on cloths, a coffin they have dressed,
out from the hallway to the yard:
Savéliyev, who polished floors.
His threadbare stripy jacket bears
a holy icon on his chest,
behind a rusty-coloured beard.
'Olga, enough now, come along.'
The washerwoman Olga's strong
right hand is grabbing at the railing
and she emerges, crying out
beside the other women wailing,
moving slowly from the court;
through the barbed agave garden
past the gate they take their burden;
the parquet shiner's curly hair
floats in the blue-skied open air.
To keep the dream before it's gone
I, too, walk by the olive trees
behind their ghostly threnodies,
stumbling around on foreign stone.

\*

The motorcycle's throaty trill
thrusts us away. The headlamp's beam
is flickering round the cliff-edge sill,

За нами следом побежал.
Сорренто спит в сырых громадах.
Мы шумно ворвались туда
И стали. Слышно, как вода
В далеких плещет водопадах.
В Страстную пятницу всегда
На глаз приметно мир пустеет,
Айдесский, древний ветер веет,
И ущербляется луна.
Сегодня в облаках она.
Тускнеют улицы сырые.
Одна ночная остерия
Огнями желтыми горит.
Ее взлохмаченный хозяин,
Облокотившись, полуспит.
А между тем уже с окраин
Глухое пение летит,
И озаряется свечами
Кривая улица вдали;
Как черный парус, меж домами
Большое знамя пронесли
С тяжеловесными кистями;
И чтобы видеть мы могли
Воочию всю ту седмицу,
Проносят плеть, и багряницу,
Терновый скорченный венок,
Гвоздей заржавленных пучок,
И лестницу, и молоток.

Но пенье ближе и слышнее.
Толпа колышется, чернея,
А над толпою лишь Она,
Кольцом огней озарена,
В шелках и розах утопая,
С недвижной благостью в лице,
В недосягаемом венце,
Плывет, высокая, прямая,
Ладонь к ладони прижимая,
И держит ручкой восковой
Для слез платочек кружевной.
Но жалкою людскою дрожью
Не дрогнут ясные черты.

while the reverberating boom
behind us echoes down the trail.
Sorrento sleeps in jumbled piles:
we burst towards it throbbing till
we've stopped. Now you can hear for miles
the splashing of the waterfalls.
Good Friday always seems to show
a visibly abandoned world.
The ancient wind of Hell blows through,
the moon's already past the full:
tonight she's in the clouds, and veiled.
The streets are growing dim and damp.
One restaurant stays up late to keep
an open door, a yellow lamp,
and the padrone half-asleep
propped on his elbows, hair dishevelled.
Across the town from further out,
muffled singing voices float.
Along the windings of the street
and lit by candles all the way
a black and sail-like banner rises,
moving in between the houses
as its ponderous tassels sway;
to show us Holy Week complete
they bring the lash, the purple gown,
the thorns contorted in a crown,
the ladder, bunch of rusty nails,
and hammer that will tamp them down.

The sound of singing now prevails.
The crowd in shadow moves as one;
above the crowd, Herself alone
illumined in a ring of fire
with silks and roses smothering her,
the features of her changeless face
crowned with serene and far-off grace
as lofty, upright, floating there
she clasps her waxen palms in prayer,
holding for her tears of grief
a lacy-bordered handkerchief.
But at the people's trembling fears

Не оттого ль к Ее подножью
Летят молитвы и мечты,
Любви кощунственные розы
И от великой полноты –
Сладчайшие людские слезы?
К порогу вышел своему
Седой хозяин остерии.
Он улыбается Марии.
Мария! Улыбнись ему!

Но мимо: уж Она в соборе
В снопах огней, в гремящем хоре.
Над поредевшею толпой
Порхает отсвет голубой.
Яснее проступают лица,
Как бы напудрены зарей.
Над островерхою горой
Переливается Денница. . .

\*

Мотоциклетка под скалой
Летит извилистым полетом,
И с каждым новым поворотом
Залив просторней предо мной.
Горя зарей и ветром вея,
Он всё волшебней, всё живее.
Когда несемся мы правее,
Бегут налево берега,
Мы повернем – и величаво
Их позлащенная дуга
Начнет развертываться вправо.
В тумане Прочида лежит,
Везувий к северу дымит.
Запятнан площадною славой,
Он всё торжествен и велик
В своей хламиде темно-ржавой,
Сто раз прожженной и дырявой.
Но вот – румяный луч проник
Сквозь отдаленные туманы.
Встает Неаполь из паров,

her lucid features do not move,
high on her plinth: which it appears
is why their prayers and wishes fly
in blasphemous roses with their love,
and overflowingly they cry
the sweetest of all human tears.
My grey-haired restaurateur, meanwhile,
has come to stand outside his doorway
where he looks and smiles at Mary.
Mary! Grant this man a smile!

By now she's entering the church
with candles like a blazing torch;
the choir resounds; the crowds break up
beneath a flickering pale blue glow
where people's faces start to show,
as dawn has powdered them with light.
Above the mountain's jagged top
the morning star is shimmering bright.

*

The motorbike comes round the cliffs,
flying in complicated twists;
at each new turning I can see
the widening bay in front of me,
burnished with dawn and brushed with wind,
ever more magical and alive.
When we skim the right-hand bend
the left-hand shoreline wheels around;
and then we swing about and drive
it back, to let the bay unfold
majestically its arc of gold.
Procida lies beneath a fog;
northward Vesuvius veiled in smoke;
with vulgar fame he may be stained
but still he stands there, solemn, grand,
dressed in his dark and rusty cloak
burnt through a hundred times or more.
But – rosy light begins to poke
through where there was a fog before.

И заиграл огонь стеклянный
Береговых его домов.

Я вижу светлые просторы,
Плывут сады, поляны, горы,
А в них, сквозь них и между них –
Опять, как на неверном снимке,
Весь в очертаниях сквозных,
Как был тогда, в студеной дымке,
В ноябрьской утренней заре,
На восьмигранном острие,
Золотокрылый ангел розов
И неподвижен – а над ним
Вороньи стаи, дым морозов,
Давно рассеявшийся дым.
И, отражен кастелламарской
Зеленоватою волной,
Огромный страж России царской
Вниз опрокинут головой.
Так отражался он Невой,
Зловещий, огненный и мрачный,
Таким явился предо мной –
Ошибка пленки неудачной.

Воспоминанье прихотливо.
Как сновидение – оно
Как будто вещей правдой живо,
Но так же дико и темно
И так же, вероятно, лживо. . .
Среди каких утрат, забот,
И после скольких эпитафий,
Теперь, воздушная, всплывет
И что закроет в свой черед
Тень соррентинских фотографий?

*5 марта 1925*
*Sorrento*
*27 февраля 1926*
*Chaville*

Naples rising from the steam
strikes up a glassy light, to gleam
from houses out along the shore.

In front of me, the radiant spaces,
hills, glades, gardens, floating places;
in them, through them and between –
another unreal photo, drawn
in outlines, a transparent dawn
as then it was, in frosty haze
on one of those November days:
there on the spire that has eight sides
the angel with gold wings presides
rosy and motionless, while crows
flock over him in frosty mist –
that mist so long-ago dispersed.
In greenish waves Castellammare
shows reflected in its mirror
Imperial Russia's towering guard
with downward-pointing head, reversed,
as in the Neva he appeared
ominous, fiery, of the night;
so was he present to my sight –
a photograph not taken right.

Memory is capricious, like
the visions that appear in dreams
and so alive, so true it seems
but yet so shadowy, wild and dark,
it seems it has to be a lie.
Among such trouble, loss and care,
after how many epitaphs,
when it emerges light as air,
what will be overtaken by
the shade of Sorrento photographs?

*5 March 1925*
*Sorrento*
*27 February 1926*
*Chaville*

## ПЕРЕД ЗЕРКАЛОМ

*Nel mezzo del cammin di nostra vita.*

Я, я, я. Что за дикое слово!
Неужели вон тот – это я?
Разве мама любила такого,
Желто-серого, полуседого
И всезнающего, как змея?

Разве мальчик, в Останкине летом
Танцевавший на дачных балах, –
Это я, тот, кто каждым ответом
Желторотым внушает поэтам
Отвращение, злобу и страх?

Разве тот, кто в полночные споры
Всю мальчишечью вкладывал прыть, –
Это я, тот же самый, который
На трагические разговоры
Научился молчать и шутить?

Впрочем – так и всегда на средине
Рокового земного пути:
От ничтожной причины – к причине,
А глядишь – заплутался в пустыне,
И своих же следов не найти.

Да, меня не пантера прыжками
На парижский чердак загнала.
И Виргилия нет за плечами, –
Только есть одиночество – в раме
Говорящего правду стекла.

*18–23 июля 1924*
*Париж*

# In Front of the Mirror

*Nel mezzo del cammin di nostra vita.*

Me, me, me. What a preposterous word!
Can that man there really be me?
Did Mama really love this face,
dull yellow with greying edges
like an ancient know-it-all snake?

Can the boy who danced in summer
at the Ostánkino country-house balls
be myself, whose every response
to freshly-hatched poets inspires
their loathing, malice and fear?

Can that youthful energy thrown into
arguing full pelt well after midnight
have been my own, now that I've learnt
when conversation turns to tragedy
better say nothing – or make a joke?

But that's how it always is at the mid-
point of following your fate on earth:
from one worthless cause to another,
and look, you've wandered away from the path
and can't even trace your own tracks.

Well, there was no leaping panther
chasing me up to my Paris garret,
and there's no Virgil at my shoulder –
there's only my singular self in the frame
of the talking, truthtelling looking-glass.

*18–23 July 1924*
*Paris*

## БАЛЛАДА

Мне невозможно быть собой,
Мне хочется сойти с ума,
Когда с беременной женой
Идет безрукий в синема.

Мне лиру ангел подает,
Мне мир прозрачен, как стекло, –
А он сейчас разинет рот
Пред идиотствами Шарло.

За что свой незаметный век
Влачит в неравенстве таком
Беззлобный, смирный человек
С опустошенным рукавом?

Мне хочется сойти с ума,
Когда с беременной женой
Безрукий прочь из синема
Идет по улице домой.

Ремянный бич я достаю
С протяжным окриком тогда
И ангелов наотмашь бью,
И ангелы сквозь провода

Взлетают в городскую высь.
Так с венетийских площадей
Пугливо голуби неслись
От ног возлюбленной моей.

Тогда, прилично шляпу сняв,
К безрукому я подхожу,
Тихонько трогаю рукав
И речь такую завожу:

# Ballad of the One-Armed Man

I think I'm going to lose my mind,
I ask myself what is the use:
a one-armed man and his pregnant wife
have gone into the picture-house.

An angel offers me the lyre,
I see the world transparently –
while he is gaping open-mouthed
at Charlie Chaplin's idiocy.

Why should he drag his little life
on such unequal terms, to live
merely a meek and unassuming
man with a folded-over sleeve?

I think I'm going to lose my mind
as pregnant wife and one-armed man
come back out of the picture-house
to walk the street for home again.

I go to fetch my leather whip
and with a long and drawn-out cry
I swing it at the angelic host,
and through the telegraph wires they fly,

bursting above the city's heights
as frightened pigeons flew above
the square in Venice once, before
the advancing footsteps of my love.

Then I approach the one-armed man,
politely taking off my hat;
I gently touch him on the sleeve
while striking up this friendly chat:

«Pardon, monsieur, когда в аду
За жизнь надменную мою
Я казнь достойную найду,
А вы с супругою в раю

Спокойно будете витать,
Юдоль земную созерцать,
Напевы дивные внимать,
Крылами белыми сиять, –

Тогда с прохладнейших высот
Мне сбросьте перышко одно:
Пускай снежинкой упадет
На грудь спаленную оно».

Стоит безрукий предо мной
И улыбается слегка,
И удаляется с женой,
Не приподнявши котелка.

*Париж, июнь – 17 августа 1925*
*Meudon*

'*Pardon monsieur*, when I'm in hell
and paying for my arrogant life
with fitting punishment, and you're
in heaven with your lady wife –

floating in peaceful contemplation
over this vale of sorrowful things,
hearing celestial harmonies
and shining with your snow-white wings

– drop from your cool abode on high
one tiny feather down to me,
a snowflake falling on this breast
that's roasting for eternity.'

The one-armed man stands facing me
and offers me a little smile,
then shuffles onward with his wife,
his bowler hat on all the while.

*Paris, June – 17 August 1925*
*Meudon*

## ЗВЕЗДЫ

Вверху – грошовый дом свиданий.
Внизу – в грошовом «Казино»
Расселись зрители. Темно.
Пора щипков и ожиданий.
Тот захихикал, тот зевнул. . .
Но неудачник облыселый
Высоко палочкой взмахнул.
Открылись темные пределы,
И вот – сквозь дым табачных туч –
Прожектора зеленый луч.
На авансцене, в полумраке,
Раскрыв золотозубый рот,
Румяный хахаль в шапокляке
О звездах песенку поет.
И под двуспальные напевы
На полинялый небосвод
Ведут сомнительные девы
Свой непотребный хоровод.
Сквозь облака, по сферам райским
(Улыбочки туда-сюда)
С каким-то веером китайским
Плывет Полярная Звезда.
За ней вприпрыжку поспешая,
Та пожирней, та похудей,
Семь звезд – Медведица Большая –
Трясут четырнадцать грудей.
И, до последнего раздета,
Горя брильянтовой косой,
Вдруг жидколягая комета
Выносится перед толпой.
Глядят солдаты и портные
На рассусаленный сумбур,
Играют сгустки жировые
На бедрах Étoile d'amour,

# The Stars

Upstairs for the cheap encounters,
downstairs for the cabaret:
in the dark the audience settle,
eager to be swept away.

Someone titters, someone yawns. . .
A nobody with thinning hair
lifts his baton, waggles it,
the hem of darkness lifts, and there –

opera-hatted, showing through
tobacco fog in spotlit green –
a red-faced pimp with teeth of gold
croons about stars, to set the scene.

And to his bedroom melody,
before a cloth of faded heavens,
dancing a risqué ring-a-roses
enter some questionable maidens.

Smiling nicely this way, that way,
through the cloudy heavenly sphere
behind some kind of Chinese fan,
let the Pole Star now appear.

Trotting behind, her chorines hurry
(some are fat and some are lean):
Ursa Major, the seven stars,
flash their breasts – which make fourteen.

And now, almost completely naked,
trailing her diamanté hair
comes an unexpected comet
straggling, kicking everywhere.

Soldiers, sailors, tailors gaze
at tinselled chaos, fix their eyes
on where Étoile d'Amour displays

Несутся звезды в пляске, в тряске,
Звучит оркестр, поет дурак,
Летят алмазные подвязки
Из мрака в свет, из света в мрак.
И заходя в дыру всё ту же,
И восходя на небосклон, –
Так вот в какой постыдной луже
Твой День Четвертый отражен!..
Не легкий труд, о Боже правый,
Всю жизнь воссоздавать мечтой
Твой мир, горящий звездной славой
И первозданною красой.

*23 сентября 1925*
*Париж*
*19 октября 1925*
*Chaville*

her rolling spotted fatty thighs;
on where the stars go skipping, tripping;
the band goes toot, the song is sung;
between the brightness and the darkness
garters glittering, snapped and flung.

Looking upwards from this gutter
from the horizon to the stars
at God's fourth day of his creation,
ah, what a shameful swamp is ours!

A hopeless task, O God our Father
in this lifetime to express
thy starry universe in glory
and the primordial loveliness.

*23 September 1925*
*Paris*
*19 October 1925*
*Chaville*

* * *

Я родился в Москве. Я дыма
Над польской кровлей не видал,
И ладанки с землей родимой
Мне мой отец не завещал.

России — пасынок, а Польше —
Не знаю сам, кто Польше я.
Но: восемь томиков, не больше, —
И в них вся родина моя.

Вам — под ярмо ль подставить выю
Иль жить в изгнании, в тоске.
А я с собой свою Россию
В дорожном уношу мешке.

Вам нужен прах отчизны грубый,
А я где б ни был — шепчут мне
Арапские святые губы
О небывалой стороне.

*25 апреля 1923*
*Saarow*

* * *

I was born in Moscow, saw
no smoke above a Polish roof,
and my father left to me
no locket of his native earth.

Stepson to Russia; but to Poland –
what could I claim of Poland's love?
My homeland? Those collected works
in eight small volumes – all I have.

For you: the neck beneath the yoke,
or else a life of yearning exile.
I can carry my own Russia
travelling with me in my holdall.

You must touch your native dust:
but wherever I may be
a sacred pair of Moorish lips
whispers the fabled land to me.

*25 April 1923*
*Saarow*

* * *

Пока душа в порыве юном,
Ее безгрешно обнажи,
Бесстрашно вверь болтливым струнам
Ее святые мятежи.

Будь нетерпим и ненавистен,
Провозглашая и трубя
Завоеванья новых истин, –
Они ведь новы для тебя.

Потом, когда в своем наитье
Разочаруешься слегка,
Воспой простое чаепитье,
Пыльцу на крыльях мотылька.

Твори уверенно и стройно,
Слова послушливые гни,
И мир, обдуманный спокойно,
Благослови иль прокляни.

А под конец узнай, как чудно
Всё вдруг по-новому понять,
Как упоительно и трудно,
Привыкши к слову, – замолчать.

*22 августа 1924*
*Holywood*

\* \* \*

While your soul bursts out in youth
uncover her, in innocence:
commit to streams of fearless talk
her holiest rebellions.

Intolerant and intolerable,
trumpet the conquests of the new,
proclaim the freshly-minted truths –
at least, these truths are new to you.

Then when your inspiration seems
a little dull, a little dry,
sing of a simple cup of tea,
a pollen-dusted butterfly.

Compose with sureness, make it shapely,
bend to your will the obedient word,
and when you've come to weigh it calmly,
you may bless or curse the world.

But there's a new and magic truth
you'll find when you're no longer young:
how thrilling and how difficult,
to live by words but hold your tongue.

*22 August 1924*
*Holywood [near Belfast]*

* * *

Нет ничего прекрасней и привольней,
Чем навсегда с возлюбленной расстаться
И выйти из вокзала одному.
По-новому тогда перед тобою
Дворцы венецианские предстанут.
Помедли на ступенях, а потом
Сядь в гондолу. К Риальто подплывая,
Вдохни свободно запах рыбы, масла
Прогорклого и овощей лежалых,
И вспомни без раскаянья, что поезд
Уж Мэстре, вероятно, миновал.
Потом зайди в лавчонку banco lotto,
Поставь на семь, четырнадцать и сорок,
Пройдись по Мерчерии, пообедай
С бутылкою «Вальполичелла». В девять
Переоденься, и явись на Пьяцце,
И под финал волшебной увертюры
«Тангейзера» – подумай: «Уж теперь
Она проехала Понтеббу». Как привольно!
На сердце и свежо и горьковато.

*[1925–1926]*

\* \* \*

Nothing more lovely and more liberating
than to part forever from your lover
and walk out of the station on your own.
The palaces of Venice then begin
a new way to present themselves before you.
Linger on a stairway for a while, then
take a gondola. Floating to the Rialto,
idly sniff the fishy smell, the butter
turning rancid, and the old stale vegetables;
remember, unregretfully, the train
most likely has already gone through Mestre.
And then call by the banco lotto kiosk,
place your bets on seven, fourteen, and forty;
proceeding through the Merceria, dine
with a bottle of Valpolicella. Nine o'clock:
change; make your appearance at the Piazza,
when at the finale of the enchanting
Tannhäuser overture, the thought will come:
'By now she's passed Pontebba.' Liberation!
Your heart is both refreshed, and slightly bitter.

*[1925–1926]*

* * *

Сквозь дикий грохот катастроф
Твой чистый голос, милый зов
Душа услышала когда-то. . .

Нет, не понять, не разгадать:
Проклятье или благодать, –
Но петь и гибнуть нам дано,
И песня с гибелью – одно.
Когда и лучшие мгновенья
Мы в жертву звукам отдаем –
Что ж? Погибаем мы от пенья
Или от гибели поем?

А нам простого счастья нет.
Тому, что с песней рождено,
Погибнуть в песне суждено. . .

*[1926–1927]*

ПАМЯТНИК

Во мне конец, во мне начало.
Мной совершенное так мало!
Но всё ж я прочное звено:
Мне это счастие дано.

В России новой, но великой,
Поставят идол мой двуликий
На перекрестке двух дорог,
Где время, ветер и песок. . .

*28 января 1928*
*Париж*

* * *

Through each disaster's crashing fall,
my dear vocation, at your call
the soul has heard your voice, so pure. . .

No, not to comprehend or guess,
to damn to hell or else to bless –
to sing and die is why we came:
song and destruction are the same.
Even the finest spots of time
we give as sacrifice to rhyme –
so do we die because we sing,
or sing because we're perishing?

For us there is no simple joy.
Whatever has been born from song
will find its fate to die in song. . .

*[1926–1927]*

# Monument

In me it ends, as it's begun.
So little made, so little done!
But I've been happy to maintain
my link in the unbroken chain.

In Russia's new but greater place
they'll put my idol's double face
where two roads cross, and there I'll stand
meeting the time, the wind, the sand. . .

*28 January 1928*
*Paris*

## ДАКТИЛИ

### 1

Был мой отец шестипалым. По ткани, натянутой туго,
   Бруни его обучал мягкою кистью водить.
Там, где фиванские сфинксы друг другу в глаза загляделись,
   В летнем пальтишке зимой перебегал он Неву.
А на Литву возвратясь, веселый и нищий художник,
   Много он там расписал польских и русских церквей.

### 2

Был мой отец шестипалым. Такими родятся счастливцы.
   Там, где груши стоят подле зеленой межи,
Там, где Вилия в Неман лазурные воды уносит,
   В бедной, бедной семье встретил он счастье свое.
В детстве я видел в комоде фату и туфельки мамы.
   Мама! Молитва, любовь, верность и смерть – это ты!

### 3

Был мой отец шестипалым. Бывало, в сороку-ворону
   Станем играть вечерком, сев на любимый диван.
Вот, на отцовской руке старательно я загибаю
   Пальцы один за другим – пять. А шестой – это я.
Шестеро было детей. И вправду: он тяжкой работой
   Тех пятерых прокормил – только меня не успел.

### 4

Был мой отец шестипалым. Как маленький лишний мизинец
   Прятать он ловко умел в левой зажатой руке,
Так и в душе навсегда затаил незаметно, подспудно
   Память о прошлом своем, скорбь о святом ремесле.
Ставши купцом по нужде – никогда ни намеком, ни словом
   Не поминал, не роптал. Только любил помолчать.

# The Dactyls

### 1

He had six fingers, my father. Across the stretch of canvas,
    Bruni tutored the soft trail of his brush.
Where the Academy sphinxes have stared each other out, he would
    dash in a summer jacket across the frozen Neva.
He returned to Lithuania, the cheerfully penniless painter
    of murals in many churches, Polish and Russian.

### 2

He had six fingers, my father. That kind of birth is lucky.
    Where the pear trees are standing on the green boundary,
the Viliya bringing its azure waters into the Neman,
    he met his joy in the poorest of poor families.
As a child I found in a drawer Mama's veil and bridal slippers.
    Mama! To me you are prayers; love; faithfulness; death.

### 3

He had six fingers, my father. We would play at 'Master Magpie'
    of an evening on the divan that we loved. That's when
I would painstakingly fold his fatherly fingers over,
    one by one – that's five. And the sixth one is me.
Half a dozen children. And truly, by hard work he brought
    five up to adulthood, but he didn't last into mine.

### 4

He had six fingers, my father. That tiny superfluous pinky
    he could hide neatly inside the fist of his left,
and inside his soul for ever, unmentioned under a bushel,
    he would hide his past, his grief for his sacred craft.
He went into business out of need, not a hint or a word
    of a memory, a murmur. He liked just to say nothing.

## 5

Был мой отец шестипалым. В сухой и красивой ладони
    Сколько он красок и черт спрятал, зажал, затаил?
Мир созерцает художник – и судит, и дерзкою волей,
    Демонской волей творца – свой созидает, иной.
Он же очи смежил, муштабель и кисти оставил,
    Не созидал, не судил. . . Трудный и сладкий удел!

## 6

Был мой отец шестипалым. А сын? Ни смиренного сердца,
    Ни многодетной семьи, ни шестипалой руки
Не унаследовал он. Как игрок на неверную карту,
    Ставит на слово, на звук – душу свою и судьбу. . .
Ныне, в январскую ночь, во хмелю, шестипалым размером
    И шестипалой строфой сын поминает отца.

*Январь 1927 – 3 марта 1928*
*Париж*


* * *


Сквозь уютное солнце апреля –
Неуютный такой холодок.
И – смерчом по дорожке песок,
И – смолкает скворец-пустомеля.


Там над северным краем земли
Черно-серая вздутая туча.
Котелки поплотней нахлобуча,
Попроворней два франта пошли.


И под шум градобойного гула –
В сердце гордом, веселом и злом:
«Это молнии *нашей* излом,
Это *наша* весна допорхнула!»


*21 апреля 1937*
*Париж*

5

He had six fingers, my father. How many streaks of paint did he
    tightly conceal in his dry and handsome palm?
The artist considers the world – judges it, and with a bold
    will, the will of his demon, creates a new one.
But he had closed his eyes, his painting gear put away,
    not to create or to judge. . . the hard, sweet vocation!

6

He had six fingers, my father. His son? He has inherited
    neither the humble heart, the brood of children,
nor the six fingers. Like placing a bet on a dubious card
    he stakes his soul, his fate, on a word, on a sound.
Now on a January night, drunken with six-fingered metre and
    six-fingered verses, the son remembers his father.

*January 1927 – 3 March 1928*
*Paris*

\* \* \*

Through the consoling April sun
the breeze, so very unconsoling,
a sandy whirlwind on the road –
shutting up the chattering starling.

Up above the northern latitudes,
dark grey clouds are bulking high.
Bowler hats get pulled down tight –
but these two dandies let theirs fly.

And under the noise of the rumbling hail,
the proud and wicked heart revives:
'That's our very own lightning crack,
the wingbeat as our spring arrives!'

*21 April 1937*
*Paris*

* * *

Не ямбом ли четырехстопным,
Заветным ямбом, допотопным?
О чем, как не о нем самом –
О благодатном ямбе том?

С высот надзвездной Музикии
К нам ангелами занесен,
Он крепче всех твердынь России,
Славнее всех ее знамен.

Из памяти изгрызли годы,
За что и кто в Хотине пал,
Но первый звук Хотинской оды
Нам первым криком жизни стал.

В тот день на холмы снеговые
Камена русская взошла
И дивный голос свой впервые
Далеким сестрам подала.

С тех пор в разнообразье строгом,
Как оный славный «Водопад»,
По четырем его порогам
Стихи российские кипят.

И чем сильней спадают с кручи,
Тем пенистей водоворот,
Тем сокровенней лад певучий
И выше светлых брызгов взлет –

Тех брызгов, где, как сон, повисла,
Сияя счастьем высоты,
Играя переливом смысла, –
Живая радуга мечты.

. . . . . . . . . . . . . . . . . . . . . .

Таинственна его природа,
В нем спит спондей, поет пэон,
Ему один закон – свобода,
В его свободе есть закон. . .

[1938]

* * *

Whyever not the four-foot iamb,
cherished from before the flood?
And what to sing, if not to sing
the iamb's gift, so rich and good?

The angels brought it down from heights
above the stars, where Muses dwell,
more glorious than all Russia's flags,
and stronger than a kremlin wall.

Consumed by years, the names of who
had fallen at Khotín, and why:
and yet the Ode upon Khotín
for us was life's initial cry.

That day a Russian muse arose
upon the snowy hills, and stood
to sing her first prodigious note
to all her distant sisterhood.

Since then in strict diversity,
as in the famous 'Waterfall',
across the same quartet of steps
the Russian verses foam and boil.

The more they spring from off the cliff,
the more the whirlpool twists away
more secret in its harmonies,
and higher leaps the sparkling spray –

that spray where, like a radiant dream
suspended joyfully in its height,
there plays chromatically with sense
the rainbow of ideal delight.

. . . . . . . . . . . . . . . . . . . . . . . . . . . . .

Its nature is mysterious,
where spondee sleeps and paeon sings,
one law is held within it – freedom.
Freedom is the law it brings. . .

*[1938]*

# Notes

'Nights', pp. 34–35. Most of Khodasevich's poems at this time are in a fairly conventional Symbolist mould, influenced by Valery Bryusov's ideas of Decadence, which he eventually rejected. This poem begins to suggest something more original, though the situation is imaginary and depends for its effect on the vague menace around the 'vagabond children' camping in the vast landscape, rather than the kind of specific detail that Khodasevich's mature work revels in. When he published his collected poems in 1927 he omitted his first two books *Youth* (1908) and *Happy Little House* (1914), considering them to be juvenilia.

Lidino was a country estate near Bologoye, between Moscow and Petersburg, where Khodasevich and his first wife Marina spent the summers of 1905–07.

'Precious ladies long ago', pp. 36–37. In *Eugene Onegin* chapter 2 stanza 29, Pushkin describes the enthusiasm of Tatyana and her mother for the novels of Richardson. Khodasevich invokes Saturn as god of decay and regeneration; the stars form a continually recurrent theme in his work (see for instance 'Midday' and 'The Stars').

'Evening', pp. 38–39. Khodasevich was in Genoa and Venice in 1911 at the age of twenty-five: he gradually absorbed what the Italian experience meant for him in later poems including 'An Encounter' (1918) and 'Nothing more lovely. . .' (1925–26). The agave (three syllables) is a succulent which grows a long flower stem; it recurs in 'Sorrento Photographs'.

Bethea notes this poem as showing Khodasevich's new mode as 'symbolist-becoming-ironist' with 'the urge to diffuse large concepts such as myth and romance in the personal and local' (p. 101). The last two lines of this poem provided the title *The Star above the Palm* for part of his book *Happy Little House*.

'The Way of the Seed', pp. 40–41. This opens the collection of the same title published in 1920. See Introduction (p. 13) for the pun on the poet's own name in the opening words. I found the term 'seedcorn' useful; 'grain' is the word used in the King James version of John 12:24 (and cf. 'Gold'), though I have kept 'seed' for the title. The black soil is deeply identified with southern Russia and Ukraine.

'The Acrobat', pp. 42–43. This poem was published in 1914 in the magazine *Novaya Zhizn'* (New Life) without the last two couplets; they were added in 1921, making it quite a different poem, with Khodasevich's sense of an earned poetic vocation over the intervening time.

'On Himself', pp. 44–45. Khodasevich frequently observes himself as if from outside, and depicts himself as a repellent creature (such as a snake or in this case a spider), but is able to overcome his otherwise low self-image in the affirmation of his poetic vocation, confirmed through his transcendent sense of connection with the stars.

'Dreams', pp. 46–47. The original rhymes *abab*. I felt that the shape of the Sapphics made this poem work formally in English without rhyme.

'In Petrovsky Park', pp. 48–49. Khodasevich had been seriously ill since 1915 (see 'An Episode') and in March 1916 his close friend Muni killed himself (see 'Look for Me' and note). This is not Muni's suicide – Khodasevich saw the hanged man in 1914 – but death is a prevalent theme in his poems of this time while there is also transfiguration, resurrection or at least some kind of survival in many of them.

I have usually avoided directly following repetitions like *zorko, zorko, zorko* ('sharply, sharply, sharply') in line 1 of the third stanza, as they are hard to bring off convincingly in English, but I have kept some repetitive pattern, here with variations on 'stare' instead. It was impossible to avoid echoes of 'The Walrus and the Carpenter' and 'The Ballad of Reading Gaol'.

'Smolensky Market', pp. 50–51. Khodasevich wrote: 'Out of this poem there began something like a friendship between Tsvetayeva and me. She recited it everywhere' (his manuscript note in a copy of the 1927 collected poems belonging to Berberova, now in the Beineke Library, Yale). Smolensky Market in Moscow was near Rostovsky Lane, where Khodasevich lived with his wife in a semi-basement.

'An Episode', pp. 52–55. The first of the seven substantial blank verse poems Khodasevich wrote from 1918 to 1920. Khodasevich's blank verse is strictly metrical like most Russian verse, but it would be hard to write acceptable English iambic pentameter so evenly, as it has been customary since Shakespeare's time to make frequent substitutions of trochees for iambs, and other metrical variations.

Khodasevich returns often to the theme of becoming disembodied. This near-death experience seems to describe a factual basis for what in other poems is more figurative or imagined. Written in the winter following the Revolution, this description of death and a painful revival continues the theme of 'The Way of the Seed' of a few weeks earlier.

'A Variation', pp. 56–57. Although this poem was written more than eighteen months later than 'An Episode', the title directly links the two.

'Gold', pp. 58–59. Around this time, Khodasevich was paying homage to his Polish background by working on translations from Polish writers, including Zygmunt Krasiński 1812–59); the epigraph is from his drama *Irydion*. The original elegiac couplets rhyme. I have used the word 'corn' as in British usage, with the generic meaning that in America is carried by 'grain', and not the specific meaning of sweetcorn or maize.

'Look for Me', pp. 60–61. This is a poem for Khodasevich's close friend Muni (Samuil Viktorovich Kissin), who committed suicide in March 1916. At that time Muni was in the army, stationed at Minsk, where he had returned after some coolness between them. Bethea's biography implies that by then Khodasevich was convalescing in the Crimea, but in his literary memoirs *Nekropol*, Khodasevich says that Muni on his last night in Moscow refused to come to his poetry reading. He describes there how the two had spent many late nights together walking the streets of Moscow, 'as though lovers escorting each other home'; he had been saved from suicide by Muni in 1911, and reproached himself terribly for being unable to save his friend in return.

The date of the poem from the end of 1917 is notable, evoking spring light at the darkest time of year and in the immediate aftermath of the Revolution: Khodasevich must have felt a great need of his companion at this time. Bethea (p. 137) considers that he was also energized in his writing at this period by his translations of poets writing in Hebrew, especially Shaul Tchernichovsky.

I have translated *svet* in the first line as 'air' rather than 'light', partly for the half-rhyme with 'floor' and partly to avoid clashing with the other meaning of 'light' in the fourth line. In the third line I have substituted 'breath' for the more literal 'sigh' to avoid the unsubtle 'a sound, a sigh, a sunray' for Khodasevich's more complex alliteration *Ya zvuk, ya vzdokh, ya zaychik*. Line 4 has an extra foot in Russian; I have not been able to reproduce the rallentando effect satisfactorily in English.

There is a manuscript in the Russian State Literary Archives opening with another stanza (Malmstad and Hughes, p. 393), which literally translates as

> Here is my room. Obstinate and capricious,
> a ray is gilding the edges of my things.
> Here is a lamp, a table, and on the wall – Derzhavin.
> Here is the mirror, but in it – I am not reflected.

This might even suggest that the speaker of the poem is to be identified with a disembodied Khodasevich, but the ambiguity there becomes rather vertiginous, and in any case the final three-stanza poem in Muni's voice is more effective and moving.

'2nd November', pp. 62–67. Khodasevich's depiction of the Revolution through concentrating on the detail of ordinary Russians' lives is part of finding his own route to modernism, as a way out of Symbolist vagueness. He was a friend of the Formalist critic Viktor Shklovsky, who developed the theory of *ostranenye* or 'making strange' – that art was to 'make the stone stony' – although he did not identify himself with Formalism. Angela Brintlinger describes his ambivalent relationship with it:

> Khodasevich himself believed strongly that form and content, like life and art, could and should never be separated. His lifelong frustration with formalists and formalism centered around their attempts to turn literary criticism into a 'science'. But in his own studies of Pushkin, especially in the essays of *Pushkin's Poetic Economy* (1924) and the later book *About Pushkin* (1937), his analyses of sound patterns, recurrent motifs, and syntactic constructions are virtually formalist in nature.

(*Pushkin Review*, vol. 6/7, 2003–04)

Michael Wachtel (*The Development of Russian Verse*, p. 95) remarks that Moscow after the Revolution is here described with phrases and imagery used by Pushkin to describe Petersburg after the flood in *The Bronze Horseman*. The friends the poet visited in the aftermath were the Pushkin scholar Mikhail Gershenzon and his family. The miniature blank verse drama *Mozart and Salieri* and narrative poem *The Gypsies* are among the major works of Pushkin, whom Khodasevich constantly studied.

'Midday', pp. 68–71. This poem looks back to Khodasevich's visit in 1911 to Venice, and has his recurrent theme of the connection between the earth and stars despite their distance.

In the third line of the second paragraph I have risked a 'porkpie' hat for *krugloy* which simply means 'round', not quite a specific enough word in English: in several other poems Khodasevich refers explicitly to a bowler hat (*kotelok*), so I don't think he means a bowler in this case.

'An Encounter', pp. 72–75. Again about the Venice trip in 1911, where the affair with Zhenya Muratova ended (see 'Nothing more lovely. . .' written in 1925–26), and the change it made in Khodasevich, then aged twenty-five; the sixteen-year-old girl is the vehicle for something more than 'being in love'. For present-day Anglophone readers an expression like 'it is our destiny as poets. . .' may seem almost repellent, but it is not possible to understand him unless we accept that like other Russian poets Khodasevich does take himself seriously in this role.

I have introduced a break after 'flow of the wine'.

'The Monkey', pp. 76–79. The perspective on public events through concentration on personal experience and detail is taken even further than in '2nd November'.

'The House', pp. 80–83. Michael Wachtel discusses this poem at length (*The Development of Russian Verse*, pp. 96–103), as the blank verse poem that Khodasevich modelled most closely on Pushkin's 'Again I visited. . .'. David Bethea (p. 184) notes that Viktor Shklovsky used the lines I have translated

> And the heart flutters
>
> like the flag aloft on the mast of a ship,
>
> between the recollection and the hope
>
> – that memory of a future. . .

as the epigraph to his memoirs *Vstrechi* (*Encounters*), published in Moscow in 1944: but he ascribed the lines to Batyushkov (1787–1855), thereby avoiding mention of the émigré Khodasevich while offering him a secret compliment.

I made *mor* in the fifth line above the break into both plague and famine – it seems able to cover both and I needed more syllables. *Paklya* in the final paragraph is as unfamiliar a word now in Russian as 'oakum' in English, but it is part of the fabric of a traditional house. 'Stove', the last word of the poem, lacks the centrality of 'hearth' to the home; but 'hearth' seems too specifically the seat of the fire to convey how the whole structure of a Russian house would be built around it.

'Without a Word', pp. 84–85. Written to Khodasevich's second wife Anna (Anyuta).

'The Dove', pp. 86–87. Not included in Khodasevich's collections, but more appropriately placed here at the end of the poems from *The Way of the Seed* than with later uncollected poems. See also the doves in '2nd November', as well as other birds in Khodasevich's poems, such as 'The Swallows'.

'I know the coffin-craftsman's working', pp. 86–87. An unpublished and apparently unfinished poem from the same material as '2nd November' and 'The Dove'.

'The Music', pp. 88–91. The opening poem of the collection *The Heavy Lyre* (1922). There seems to be no standard English expression for what I have called 'frost vapour' (line 7); this is from sublimation, where the water in the snow is converted directly from a solid to a gaseous state through the action of sunshine. It is the same process as the effect of the 'smoke' from dry ice (frozen carbon dioxide).

'Lady's washed her hands so long', pp. 90–91. This expresses Khodasevich's deep-seated guilt over the suicide of his friend Muni in 1916 (see 'Look for Me').

'Not my mother. . .', pp. 92–95. The first four stanzas date from 1917. Khoda-sevich found this a difficult poem to write, and originally there was a straight-forwardly patriotic fifth stanza without the dilemma of loving and cursing. Khodasevich returned to the poem with a sudden inspiration on 2 March 1922. Nina Berberova says: 'In haste he bought galoshes one size larger than necessary, shoved the draft of his poem in them and came to my place. A year later, in Berlin, the draft was found in one of the galoshes' (Berberova, p. 140). However, the poem was evidently already memorized. Bethea considers that the new flow of inspiration came from Khodasevich's study of how Pushkin identified his nurse with his muse.

Khodasevich's nurse was from Tula where the family had been living earlier; young Vladislav was very weak, and in order to be his nurse she gave up her own newborn son to an orphanage, where he inevitably died.

I have sacrificed a number of specific names of things and places for read-ability, such as 'Vyazemsky gingerbread' (a fruity brick-shaped speciality from the town of Vyazma); 'Mary's shrine' (fourth stanza) is the famous Iverskaya icon, where Yelena took the boy after his escape (falling out of a window, he rolled down the roof and was caught in the gutter); the 'coronation crowd' (last stanza) are the 1,389 people who were trampled to death at Khodynka when gifts were given out at the time of Nicholas II's coronation.

There is an unstated comparison with Pushkin's nurse who, by contrast, did tell the stories that grounded him in Russian folk culture. With 'thundering power' (*gromkaya derzhava*, fifth stanza) I have turned up the volume some-what: *gromkaya* is loud, famous or glorious (with a pejorative tone); again this is Pushkin, from *The Gypsies*, where Aleko says 'A son of yours, and come to this, O Rome, O city of resounding name' (Antony Wood's translation). Khodasevich is not afraid to announce his vocation, not only as poet, but as guardian of the language despite not being ethnically Russian but Polish and Jewish. The future is entirely discounted: exile is not referred to, although by March 1922 it was becoming more likely. He concentrates on the 'secret joy' (eighth stanza) residing in the grave of Yelena Kuzina, but once in exile the physical location of Russia was to become less important than the language, and Pushkin as his role model (see 'I was born in Moscow. . .').

'I love the world, its people, nature', pp. 96–97. 'The world' is my own interpo-lation to fill the line; the original is literally 'I love people, I love nature'.

Writing to Andrey Bely in August 1921, Khodasevich told him to throw out this poem because he had put it by mistake in the packet he sent (Malmstad and Hughes, p. 413); but he included it in *The Heavy Lyre*.

'To the Visitor', pp. 98–99. Written while Khodasevich was living in Dom Iskusstv or 'Disk', the House of the Arts, a former aristocratic palace on Nevsky Prospekt in Petersburg which had apartments for writers (see also 'Ballad of the Heavy Lyre'). He had been in an argument with Yekaterina Sultanova, one of his neighbours there: Malmstad and Hughes suggest he is alluding to a rule of Catherine the Great that rank and arrogance were to be left outside the door along with hats and especially swords. This was a time of great intensity not only in Khodasevich's own writing, but in his literary relationships, quite apart from the intensity of the public world. The year 1921 saw the death of Aleksandr Blok and, in August, the execution of Nikolay Gumilyov.

'Giselle', pp. 98–99. I have avoided reading rhymed translations before attempting my own, but while David Bethea's translations in *Khodasevich: His life and art* are not usually metrical and rhyming, in this case (pp. 23–24) he did include the rhymes in the even-numbered lines which I have taken on here, and I have not tried to improve on his line 2 at all. Bethea uses it in his introduction to Khodasevich's art as illustrating his 'balletic' poetry, combining 'drama and choreography, rhetorical tension and dancelike release'. Robert P. Hughes mentions that this is the last poem he wrote in Russia, on May Day 1922 with the parade outside, after he had been to *Giselle* the night before ('Khodasevich: irony and dislocation', in Karlinsky and Appel, p. 57). His art had matured but was about to move into eclipse through the frustrating years of exile.

'From the Window', pp. 100–01. Almost exactly ten years before, Khodasevich's mother had died in a street accident with a bolting horse, which must have been in his mind with the horse and the apprehension of other disasters.

'The Stopper', pp. 104–05. Khodasevich noted that this poem was meant to be longer, but he could not think how to continue it; there were four more lines which he deleted when he realized no continuation was necessary (Malmstad and Hughes, p. 420).

'The Swallows', pp. 106–07. The trapped birds here are noticeably the opposite of the freed doves in 'The Dove' and '2nd November' of three years before. The image of the swallow recurs in Russian poetry, for instance in Derzhavin, Fet and Maykov (see Bethea, pp. 230–31). Maykov was the first 'real live, genuine poet' Khodasevich met at the age of ten, when he recited the old man's 'Swallows' to him (Bethea, p. 20) – a defining moment, although Maykov was not a poet he admired later.

'Step over, leap across', pp. 108–09. I have changed Khodasevich's *pince-nez* to 'spectacles', which loses genuine detail, but I felt it would draw attention unnecessarily, and was hard to make euphonious.

'Twilight', pp. 108–09. One of the strangest of Khodasevich's poems about his ambivalence towards himself. The original is fully though irregularly rhymed, but this seemed less important for the English than usual.

'Bel'skoye Ust'ye', pp. 110–11. Bel'skoye Ust'ye was a country village with a colony for artists and writers. As in 'On Himself' and other poems, Khodasevich represents himself as the unpleasant outsider, serpent, spider or fallen angel, bringing the fogs and tuberculosis of the city to this idyllic place.

'I play at cards . . ', pp. 112–13. Khodasevich was a passionate card-player, and considered that people's styles of play said much about them. In early 1922, a time when conditions for writers were looking worse, Khodasevich and Nina Berberova were embarking on their relationship, although his commitment to her at this stage seems not to have been total: the 'maiden' in the last line may be identified with both Nina and Ophelia. He wrote to his wife Anna – who was also seeing someone else – on 3 February:

> Ophelia perished and sang [a quotation from Afanasy Fet (1820–92)] – whoever does not perish, does not sing. I say straightforwardly: I am singing and perishing. Neither you nor anybody believes me. I call out to myself – *perish*. The poor girl Berberova I will not destroy, because I am sorry for her. I have only promised to show her the path, on which people die. But, as I lead her as far as the path, I shall give her sandwiches for the return journey, and go along the path *alone*. She will ask herself on the path, is that what they all want, the little men. And then they can't stay with it.

(Malmstad and Hughes, p. 424; translation – P.D.)

Berberova herself says little about the time between New Year and April 1922, by which time 'Khodasevich told me that two tasks lay before us: to be together and survive. Or perhaps: to survive and be together' (Berberova, p. 140).

'The Automobile', pp. 114–15. Bethea notes that this exceptionally dark poem is followed in the collection *The Heavy Lyre* by a 'radiant surge of lyrics' culminating in the 'Ballad of the Heavy Lyre' itself, written only shortly afterwards.

Fifth stanza: the wings in the original are simply 'black', but I have introduced 'than a crow's' for rhyme, which seemed appropriate.

'Onto the tarnished spires', pp. 116–17. The original rhymes are couplets. Written at Dom Iskusstv, so the spires are those of Petersburg.

'I watch the humble working men', pp. 118–19. Misdroy was on the Baltic coast of Germany, and is now Międzyzdroje in Poland. The line 'You'll say: a lofty angel walks' is an allusion to 'Problesk' ('The Gleam') by Tyuchev.

'Ballad of the Heavy Lyre', pp. 120–23. This poem closes the book *The Heavy Lyre*. The original title is simply 'Ballad', but this is also the title of a later poem, which I have called 'Ballad of the One-Armed Man'. Nabokov called his version 'Orpheus', which gives away the ending unnecessarily, but to me it did need the lyre in the title to prepare the reader, in the way that Khodasevich's own book title did. His self-conscious vocation as a poet reaches its height here. In later poems (including the other 'Ballad') the frustrations of the poetic vocation do not receive this transcendent answer.

Khodasevich had a corner room at Dom Iskusstv (see also 'To the Visitor'), semicircular according to Berberova rather than 'circular'.

One translation dilemma has been the lighting at the end of the first stanza, literally 'sixteen candles'. *Svecha* can also mean 'candlepower'; Vladimir Markov and Merrill Sparks (1966) translate it as 'sixteen watts', which happens to be the strength of Edison's 1880 lightbulb; Nabokov and Bethea call it a sixty-watt bulb. Neither electricity nor candles could be reliably supplied at the time, but Nina Berberova explicitly mentions an electric bulb in the hallway (p. 134), while she also describes the downstairs 'gala' rooms where she went to a dance, with 'four-hundred-pound chandeliers' left over from the aristocrats. Smaller chandeliers seem likely also in the writers' apartments. Berberova simply quotes from the poem – 'In his window, beneath the "sixteen-candle sun". . .' – with no explanation (p. 135). It might have been an electric chandelier.

In the first stanza I have introduced 'sphere' for the rhyme: it brings in the celestial dimension a line earlier than the original, and goes with 'circular' – perhaps too neatly but in line with other elements like the gloom for the serpent to see through (ninth stanza). Other liberties taken are attempted in the spirit of the poem, and especially of the considerable tone shift from the depressive and dislocated mood at one end of the poem to heroic invocation of Orpheus at the other. Khodasevich's way with tone is particularly fascinating.

'Petersburg', pp. 124–25. Written after three and a half years of exile, this opening poem of the collection *European Night* (1927) sets the tone with its retrospect on the extraordinary period of 1921–22 and the unspoken question of what the poetic vocation can mean in exile with only a small quarrelsome audience of émigré poets. Khodasevich's personal references to his life in Petersburg are somewhat opaque, with little attempt to be comprehensible to a wider audience. In the second stanza, the 'herald-girl' is Nina Berberova, their relationship developing in the winter of 1921–22 (I have been a little free with 'took my hand' where the original is 'appeared'); 'music's concord' refers to the 'Ballad of the Heavy Lyre' in which the lyre of Orpheus is handed to him through the wind; payment at the time was often in fish, which he exchanged for other goods as his faddy diet meant he refused to eat it.

The scansion in the original is trickier than usual, with extra-metrical syllables (which I have not reproduced), and the last line of the poem is a foot short. The sudden closure of the short line helps to raise the question of what could come next in the story of his poetry. I did not attempt to rhyme lines 1 and 3 of each stanza; the rhyme of those lines in the last stanza came of its own accord and I decided not to fight it, as it may suggest the 'classic rose' maintaining its musical order, with the short last line as the Soviet disruption.

'God alive! I'm not beyond coherence', pp. 126–27. I tackled this poem early on in my acquaintance with Khodasevich and did not attempt the intricate rhyme scheme. The poem is an exasperated stand against the Futurists' 'metalogical' language, their *zaumny yazyk* (literally 'language beyond mind'). I have translated *zaumny* in the opening line as 'beyond coherence' rather than 'metalogical', to be clearer about the underlying meaning before entering into the jargon of the Futurists.

'The babble of spring. . .', pp. 128–29. Evidently a companion piece to 'God alive!. . .': later the same month Khodasevich describes his own kind of metalogical language, and relates it to his recurrent tropes of leaving the body and connecting with the stars.

'Berlin View', pp. 130–31. Berlin attracted many of the Russian exiles. The city is the setting for Nabokov's *The Gift*, in which Khodasevich is at least in part the model for the poet Koncheyev.

'At the Dachas', pp. 132–33. Gorky had a Russian-style dacha on the lake at Saarow near Berlin. The poem may include reminiscences of Russia (and Chaliapin was being recorded from 1901), but seems likely to be immediately inspired by Saarow.

'I get up weakened from my bed', pp. 134–35. The mysterious rays of radio are reminiscent of the strange electricity flowing through the poet in 'An Episode'.

'Sorrento Photographs', pp. 136–45. The irregularly rhyming tetrameter is modelled on Pushkin, in arbitrary patterns of couplets, alternating or embracing rhymes; I have rhymed, but the pattern is more irregular and sometimes more distant than that of the original.

Khodasevich and Berberova were with Gorky in Sorrento from October 1924 to April 1925; the motorcyclist was Gorky's son, also called Maksim, and Khodasevich rode in the sidecar; Maksim junior was a keen photographer. As well as being the device for evoking images of Russia, photography had a personal meaning for the poet as it was his father's profession after he gave up painting (see 'The Dactyls').

In his essay on 'Sorrento Photographs', Michael Basker says of the composition of the poem that it 'spanned a period of bitter realization that temporary emigration had irrevocably become the permanent exile Khodasevich had feared' (p. 21), and the time the poem took to get started reflected the 'crucial considerations' of the 'struggle and responsibility of writing, as well as the fate of the writer and the powerlessness to direct one's own lot'. Describing Khodasevich's 'stylistic angularities' (p. 31), Basker suggests that 'in a poem in which lack of conscious control is thematized from the outset, the stumbling awkwardnesses of syntax, flatness of construction and falling cadences

... might also be taken to suggest that, like recollection, poetic material, too, is "disobedient" to the lyric self. This in turn might be construed as a concomitant failure to sustain the literary norm of a previous era to which ... overarching form, scope, other elements of diction unmistakeably point, but which now evades the (exilic) artistic grasp.' Basker also describes the way rhymes and tetrameter lines in the poem are reminiscent of other poetry, especially Pushkin, and likens this to the 'palimpsest' effect of the overlapping photographs; other poets echoed include Gumilyov and Blok, whose deaths in 1921 marked the end of a literary age.

Gregory Woods has helped me to picture the geography of the area, which I have never visited, and I have slightly shifted the view of the Amalfi pass towards the ravine below it (for the rhyme, of course). Basker notes the echo in *Amalfitansky pereval* ('Amalfi's deep ravine', line 10 in paragraph 3) of *Admiralteyskaya igla*, the Admiralty spire in Petersburg, which similarly takes up a single tetrameter line in the prologue of Pushkin's *Bronze Horseman* – the kind of echo impossible to provide in English.

The 'agave' appears also in the 1913 poem 'Evening', from Khodasevich's 1911 trip to Italy; for Khodasevich it evidently stands for a distinctly non-Russian vegetation. The 'cloths' on which the women are carrying the coffin are *polotentsa*, usually meaning 'towels', but here special pieces of cloth also used as the bands for lowering the coffin into the grave.

Basker notes that there are two traditional processions on Good Friday in Sorrento, one before dawn, of penitents in hooded white robes, and one in the evening, in hooded black robes and with the crown of thorns and other objects from the crucifixion, as well as Christ in a coffin (not mentioned in the poem); each includes a statue of Mary but dressed differently. Khodasevich's description of early light suits the first procession, but he has incorporated elements of the second.

The morning star is associated both with the Virgin Mary and with Lucifer, and Bethea mentions (p. 311) that Berberova suggested to him this was intended; Khodasevich may no longer have been a Symbolist poet but these symbolic meanings still operate, connecting the adoration of Mary in the procession with the upside-down angel to follow. It is also yet another appearance of stars in his work.

The views that appear on the turns to right and left, Basker suggests, will evoke for a Russian reader the learned cat in Pushkin's prologue to *Ruslan and Lyudmila*, who turns to the right to produce a song, and to the left to tell a tale. The 'houses out along the shore' in Naples (*beregovykh ego domov*) are a very clear echo of a line in *The Bronze Horseman* which could be translated 'its granite along the shore', *beregovoy ego granit*.

The 'spire that has eight sides' is on the cathedral at the centre of the Peter-Paul Fortress, the heart of the foundation of Petersburg.

'In Front of the Mirror', pp. 146–47. The epigraph is from the opening of Dante's *Inferno*. Another case of Khodasevich's self-image as a snake or other unpleasant creature, as with the spider in 'On Himself' and the serpent in 'Ballad of the Heavy Lyre'.

'Ballad of the One-Armed Man', pp. 148–51. After much travelling around Europe, Khodasevich and Berberova settled in Paris in April 1925 and remained there. He revisits both the 'Ballad of the Heavy Lyre' and the Venetian experience, but now in the light of his stalled vocation as a poet; he is unable to appreciate the low culture of Chaplin, and the war-wounded French citizen is unable to appreciate his Russian poetry.

'The Stars', pp. 152–55. The last poem in *European Night*. The original is not set out in stanzas: it starts as a free-rhyming poem à la Pushkin, like 'Sorrento Photographs', but after the tenth line it is all in *abab* rhymes. I have regularized it because I wanted to suggest an echo of Eliot's quatrains as in 'Sweeney Erect', the demi-monde scenario being so appropriate.

Soldiers and tailors are in the original but not sailors (eighth stanza). It has also been hard to resist echoes of Yeats's 'cloths of heaven' (fourth stanza), and Wilde's 'We are all in the gutter, but some of us are looking at the stars' (penultimate stanza).

'I was born in Moscow...', pp. 156–57. Berberova published the first two stanzas in a memorial article after Khodasevich's death in 1939. There is also a three-stanza 1917 version of this poem, naturally without the poignancy of exile, and with recollections of family lore about Poland and Lithuania as in 'The Dactyls'.

Although his family were Lithuanian Poles, Khodasevich became thoroughly Russified through being brought up and educated in Russia (see 'Not my mother...'). As an adult he translated Polish poets into Russian (see notes to 'Gold'), and the Jewish poets who had begun writing in Hebrew, but despite maintaining an interest in those cultures, he was never able to identify as either Polish or Jewish.

The 'eight small volumes' are the works of Pushkin; and the 'Moorish lips' are Pushkin's, from his African heritage – literally 'Arab lips' in Khodasevich's Russian, but that would be too misleading in English.

'While your soul bursts out in youth', pp. 158–59. This poem is continuing thoughts about poets and poetry from an earlier time – Malmstad and Hughes note a draft from 12 May 1920; the implications of a poet holding his tongue would have changed by 1924 to the condition of exile.

'Nothing more lovely and more liberating', pp. 160–61. In this unpublished late return to blank verse, Khodasevich also returns to the Venetian trip of

1911, specifically his affair with Yevgenia Muratova. He revisited Venice in 1924.

'Through each disaster's crashing fall', pp. 162–63. A return to the theme of 'singing and perishing' (see 'I play at cards. . .'). I have rhymed with more couplets than the original, where the second half of the central section has alternating rhyme.

'Monument', pp. 162–63. The subject echoes Pushkin's version of Horace's 'Exegi monumentum', in which the poet stands up for the autonomy and greater longevity of his art, against the power of the emperor (whether Augustus or Tsar Alexander). Khodasevich is more ambiguous about his future in Soviet Russia, but is firm in his faith that he has upheld the canon of Russian poetry.

'The Dactyls', pp. 164–67. This was the poem, discussed in Michael Wachtel's chapter on classical metres in Russian, that alerted me to Khodasevich as a poet I wanted to translate. The dactyl foot (long-short-short, or stress-unstress-unstress) is literally a 'finger' in Greek. I have given the title a definite article, absent in Russian, so that the poem can refer to itself as the 'six-fingered verses' of the last stanza: some of the 'dactyls' are in fact anapaests, their mirror image, stressed on the third syllable not the first.

Wachtel describes the prosodic tradition that Khodasevich is following: 'The elegiac distich combined one line of this hexameter with a line of so-called pentameter. The classical pentameter should not be confused with more recent conceptions of this term. Like the hexameter (from which it was derived), it contained *six* long syllables'; and he notes further that 'already in classical times, the pentameter line was indented, making the elegiac distich immediately identifiable graphically. This convention, usually maintained by modern European poets, serves to "announce" the distich's presence before a single word has been read' (p. 173). For my translation I have roughly followed the English tradition of 'elegiacs' alternating our standard hexameter and pentameter, which suits the shorter words of English better, although it breaks the meaningful pattern of sixes. Khodasevich's form is not only a play on the six-fingered life of his father: 'as a consciously stylized marker of antiquity, it treats the recent past as if it were ancient history, giving a scope and power that the events recounted could otherwise not possibly attain' (Wachtel, p. 204).

This looks from our time like a 'confessional' poem, and it is written at a time of retrospection and thinking very much about the giving up of an art, 'the hard, sweet vocation' of poetry, which Khodasevich wrote less and less. But it is not straightforward autobiography. It may appear from the poem that his mother died when he was young, and his father died perhaps in his son's late adolescence, not seeing him into 'adulthood', but in fact his mother died in an accident in 1911 when Khodasevich was twenty-five years old, and his father, whose business was photography, died later the same year. That was the year in which he had already been significantly changed by the visit to Italy, and his true maturity does start once he was able to understand this change.

The Neman (second stanza) is the main river of Lithuania, and the Viliya (or Neris) is a tributary, on which Vilnius stands; they join at Kaunas. Khodasevich seems never to have visited this location, so he is drawing on family lore, but also placing his origins where the poet Mickiewicz came from. The Polish scholar W. Lednicki, writing in 1953 in the New York Russian-language journal *Opyty*, considered that lines 2 and 3 of the second stanza contain echoes of Mickiewicz's *Pan Tadeusz* and *Konrad Wallenrod*. The picture of 'the poorest of poor families' (second stanza) seems to be imaginary, as his parents' families were not in poverty. 'Master Magpie' (third stanza) is my fanciful name for *soróka-voróna* ('magpie-crow'), a finger game: it involves counting off fingers like 'This little piggy' with toes, but also has something in common with 'Round and round the garden, like a teddy bear'.

'Through the consoling April sun', pp. 166–67. By this time, two years before his death, Khodasevich was writing almost no poetry at all. Despite a sense of longing for the Russian weather, this poem just manages not to reverse his stand against longing for Russia itself: its April storms have come to him in Paris.

'Whyever not the four-foot iamb', pp. 168–69. This is the last poem Khodasevich wrote, and he left space for another stanza in the space filled with dots. The 'Ode upon Khotín' (third stanza) is by Lomonosov (1711–65), about a battle against the Turks and Tatars in 1739. 'The Waterfall' (fifth stanza) is by Derzhavin (1743–1816). These two poets established the iambic tetrameter as the classic metre of the Russian tradition, where substituted feet are less common than in English (see note to 'An Episode'), but here and throughout the translations in this book I have allowed myself some of the English kind of freedom.


P.D.

# АЛФАВИТНЫЙ УКАЗАТЕЛЬ СТИХОТВОРЕНИЙ

# INDEX OF TITLES AND FIRST LINES

VLADISLAV KHODASEVICH

Selected Poems

VLADISLAV FELITSIANOVICH KHODASEVICH (1886–1939) was born in Moscow of a Polish-Lithuanian family, with Jewish maternal grandparents. He spent his first thirty-three years in Moscow. He identified his poetic vocation at school, on leaving which he worked for some years on Symbolist literary periodicals.

His first verse collection *Youth* appeared in 1908, and his second, *Happy Little House*, in 1914. In 1919 he moved to Petersburg to work with Maksim Gorky at the House of Arts on a vast translation project popularizing world literature. In 1922, after the death of the greatest Russian poet of the time, Aleksandr Blok, and the execution of Anna Akhmatova's husband Nikolay Gumilyov, he found it impossible to work in Russia. With his partner Nina Berberova, later to become an internationally known writer, he left Russia for Berlin and the spa of Saarow, where Gorky had a dacha. After passing through Prague, Marienbad, Venice, Sorrento and Belfast, the two settled in Paris, where Khodasevich wrote less and less poetry and increasingly turned to memoirs, notably *Necropolis,* and critical studies.

Khodasevich's finest poetry is included in his collections *The Way of the Seed* (Moscow, 1920) and *The Heavy Lyre* (Moscow-Petrograd, 1922; 2nd edition Berlin, 1923) and the section 'European Night' in the first collected edition of his work (Paris, 1927). Deleted from Russian literary history in the Soviet regime because of his emigration, he is now placed firmly by Russians in the pantheon of their country's greatest modern poets.

PETER DANIELS began translating Khodasevich while holding a Hawthornden Fellowship in 2009. His own poetry has appeared in several pamphlets, and his first full collection *Counting Eggs* was published by Mulfran Press in 2012. He has won first prize in the Ledbury (2002), Arvon (2008) and TLS (2010) Poetry Competitions. He studied Russian to A level, and has pursued further Russian language studies at the University of London. He works as a freelance editor.

MICHAEL WACHTEL, professor of Slavic languages and literature at Princeton University, is the author of *The Development of Russian Verse: Meter and its Meanings* (1998), *The Cambridge Introduction to Russian Poetry* (2004) and *A Commentary to Pushkin's Lyric Poetry* (2011).